# Making News
# — in the —
# Global Market

Don M. Flournoy & Robert K. Stewart

Foreword by
## Jimmy Carter

UNIVERSITY
UP of
JL
LUTON PRESS

**British Library Cataloguing in Publication Data**
A catalogue record for this book is available from the British Library

ISBN 1 86020 517 8 (Hardback)
ISBN 1 86020 542 9 (Paperback)

Published by
John Libbey Media
Faculty of Humanities
University of Luton
75 Castle Street
Luton
Bedfordshire LU1 3AJ
United Kingdom
Telephone: +44 (0) 1582 743297; Fax: +44 (0) 1582 743298
e-mail: ulp@luton.ac.uk

Cover design by Derek Virtue, DataNet

Printed in Great Britain by Whitstable Litho Ltd, Whitstable, Kent, UK

# CNN

## Making News
## — in the —
## Global Market

# Contents

# Foreword by Jimmy Carter

Ted Turner is one of my heroes. He's the most evocative, innovative, effective, dedicated person that I have ever known in the American news media.

But it was the ocean that first introduced me to Ted, long before he became known for revolutionizing the news business. I first encountered his great determination and drive in 1977, when he came to the White House after successfully defending the America's Cup. He had overcome many setbacks in his quest for that prize, and since then, I have come to see that sailing victory as a metaphor for his career.

Back then, news accounts painted the picture of a modern-day swashbuckler, a man who was equal parts daring and guile. But the Ted Turner I have come to know in the last 15 years, spending many hours on horseback, in fishing boats, and in the privacy of our homes, has a unique persistence and passion for life. His deep and long-standing commitment to world peace, human rights and environmental quality has lead Ted into several remarkable ventures.

One of Ted's goals is to bring the peoples of the world closer together, and there is no better example than the founding of Cable News Network in 1980. CNN, the world's first live, round-the-clock, all news TV network, broke all molds of television journalism. Now seen in more than 200 countries, CNN has done more to close the gaps of misunderstanding between the world's people than any enterprise in recent memory. Ted gave life to Marshall McLuhan's prediction that television would create "a global village."

When I travel in other countries on behalf of the Carter Center, I frequently meet with Heads of State and other top officials, including the U.S. ambassadorial staff. I rarely go into any dignitary's home or office anywhere on earth that I don't find a television turned to CNN. CNN has become the pre-eminent source of accurate news reporting throughout the world, allowing people from diverse backgrounds to share their experiences. This kind of communication contributes enormously to understanding other cultures, which in turn, makes for a more benevolent and peaceful global community.

Ted, like the name of his famous sail boat, Courageous, has accomplished great things in spite of criticism, jealousy, competition, and personal and financial obstacles. In all of his endeavors, he has put his vast resources to work in the service of humanity. His commitment to the environment has been reflected in the television programs he puts on the air. His belief in the importance of cooperation has been expressed in  his international sports efforts.

As CNN has grown and evolved over the last 17 years, one of the programs I admire the most is *World Report*. *World Report* airs stories by reporters in more than 80 countries around the globe. CNN's commitment has been to broadcast these stories without editing, giving local journalists a chance to report the news they consider the most important in their countries.

It is impossible to think long about CNN or any of Ted's other enterprise before thinking about the man at their helm. Whether captaining a sleek and powerful sailboat or directing a multi-faceted communications corporation, Ted Turner manages to imprint his own personality on the whole of his organization. This book, detailing the rise and success of CNN, is a testament to the persistence and passion of a single man. Ted Turner is American's 20 century visionary.

# Authors' Preface

CNN's presence is felt in every part of the world, its brand name synonymous with news from everywhere, all the time. The same energy, boldness, and responsiveness to market opportunities that defined CNN's early years makes it today's company to watch and learn from in the business of international news.

*CNN: Making News in the Global Market* chronicles how founder Ted Turner transformed his Atlanta-based company into a credible international news service in spite of his activist social agenda that challenged well-established journalistic traditions. Furthermore, his company's aggressive strategy of covering news whenever and wherever it happens, of breaking the news first, of going live from the scene, has frequently put the company in the uncomfortable position of shaping the events it relentlessly covers.

This book uses first-hand accounts from many insiders, incorporating interviews with Ted Turner and company managers, with those who gather, produce, market and globally distribute the news, and with those who have signed on as CNN partners. The result is a revealing look at how an American company took shape around a strong leader, how it built and projected a world-class identity, and now prepares for stiff international competition.

In an attempt to provide updated information regarding our subject, we are maintaining a Web site for this book on the Ohio University Institute for Telecommunications Studies site, located at http://its.ohiou.edu/cnnbook. Also included are photographs of many of the individuals interviewed in this book, as well as corrections, clarifications, reviews, and links to Web sites that we have listed in the book.

This book would not have been possible without the help of many individuals. We would like to thank Lou Curles of CNN for facilitating our attendance at *World Report* contributors conferences over so many years, and for her guidance in navigating through the CNN maze. We also are grateful to the managers and staff of CNN's International Desk, who took the time to explain to us what they do, and why. We thank Ralph Wenge and his staff at *World Report* for their time and patience in helping us understand the unique nature of that operation. We also thank the many *World Report* contributors who responded to our questions.

We also want to thank Paolo Ghilardi, a graduate student from Italy who interned on the International Desk in 1996, for sharing in the interviewing of CNN executives. In addition we wish to thank research assistants Yu-li Chang, a *World Report* contributor from Taiwan and currently a doctoral student in the E. W. Scripps School of Journalism at Ohio University, and Sang-chul Lee and Ece Algan, doctoral students in OU's School of Telecommunications. Many other graduate students at Ohio University have been involved in our research over the years, and we wish especially to thank Rachada Kongkeo, Rani Dilawari, Charles Ganzert and Chun-il Park. We also want to thank our editor, Nancy Basmajian, who helped make the book more readable and, often, more sensible, as well as Molly Stewart, who assisted with the cover design. And finally, we thank our families for suffering the many hours that it takes to complete such a project. To our wives, Mary Anne and Candace, thanks for your support.

Don M. Flournoy and Robert K. Stewart
Ohio University

# 1

# The Rapid Rise of CNN

*It is the policy of TBS that any person, event, etc. which is not part of the United States be referred to as international rather than foreign. . . . The word foreign implies something unfamiliar and creates a perception of misunderstanding. In contrast, international means "among nations" and promotes a sense of unity.*[1]

Ted Turner dedicated the Cable News Network on June 1, 1980, calling the round-the-clock news operation "America's news channel." Using satellites to deliver CNN to cable operators around the country meant that Turner could reach American consumers without having to build a conventional network of local broadcast affiliates to rebroadcast his programs over the airwaves. Unfortunately for Turner, only about 20 percent of U.S. television households could receive cable television, and his new 24-hour news channel reached only 1.7 million of those households—far fewer than were needed to make a profit.

The pace at which Ted Turner lost money only accelerated 18 months after CNN's launch when the company created Headline News, a second 24-hour news network, to fight off a bid by ABC and Westinghouse to begin the Satellite News Channel, a competing cable news service. Predictions of a failure were common among media analysts, who wondered if Turner had sufficiently deep pockets to allow him to lose money for years to come. By the mid-1980s Turner had spent more than 70 million dollars keeping CNN and Headline News afloat.

---

[1] Ted Turner (vice chairman, Time Warner Inc.), memo to all staff (March 1990).

1

Yet, signs of a payoff were beginning to show even as Turner's debt piled up. More and more cable channels such as ESPN, HBO, Nickelodeon, Arts & Entertainment, USA, Disney, Showtime and C-SPAN—together with Turner's cable channels—were countering cable's limited penetration by making cable more attractive to viewers. By 1985, Turner's original news channel was reaching more than 33 million households—four out of five U.S. cable homes—and nearly 40 percent of all U.S. TV homes. Headline News had 18 million subscribers. These numbers were vital to CNN's economic success because larger audiences mean greater advertising revenues.

But cable changed the formula for making money in broadcasting. Even if the number of Americans watching any *single* cable program remained a fraction of the audience of the Big Three broadcast networks' nightly news shows, the cumulative effect of small but multiple (and 24-hour) revenue streams could still generate operating profits. Such providers could charge cable companies a per user fee for each cable subscriber, giving them an important second stream of revenue. CNN's two news channels were proving that news programming could make money in a world of splintered television audiences:

> [In 1985] CNN generated $56.5 million in advertising revenues, up 23.3%. CNN Headline News also more than doubled its flagging advertising revenues in 1985 to $13.7 million from $6.4 million. Operating profit for the cable segment did an about-face in 1985, posting an $18.8 million gain compared with a $15.3 million loss the prior year.[2]

By the mid-1980s, CNN and Headline News were fast becoming important parts of a growing family of networks making up the Turner Broadcasting System. Shortly after Turner's failed bid that same year to buy CBS, which would have vastly increased the audience for CNN programming, Turner returned to the strategy of expanding audience through the creation of still more cable-based news and entertainment networks. The global market appeared to offer new opportunities for growth, what with the explosive growth in international trade and shifts in the world markets, all of which were creating demands for more up-to-date

---

[2] "Buyouts Shuffle 1985 Media Rankings," *Advertising Age* (30 June 1986): S-4.

information. For Turner, it was a relatively simple matter to combine the CNN and Headline News domestic signals and put them on an international satellite in 1985, thus creating CNN International.[3]

Since the mid-1980s, the CNN family of networks has grown to include nearly a dozen news channels and a wholesale news service (CNN Newsource) that sells video news to approximately 600 broadcast affiliates worldwide.[4] With so many 24-hour news networks and services, CNN today has an insatiable demand for programming. The key to survival and success is simple: take any given news item and air it again and again in different ways on each of the company's networks. In CNN's centralized newsgath-

| CNN Networks | Launch Year |
| --- | --- |
| CNN | 1980 |
| CNN Headline News | 1981 |
| CNN Radio | 1982 |
| CNN International | 1985 |
| CNN *World Report* news exchange | 1987 |
| CNN Newsource | 1987 |
| Noticiero Telemundo-CNN | 1988 |
| CNN Airport Network | 1992 |
| CNN Interactive (Internet) | 1995 |
| CNN*fn* | 1995 |
| CNN–SI (Sports Illustrated) | 1996 |
| CNN en Español | 1997 |

ering operation, a team at CNN's International Desk assigns stories to the network's reporters, and the resulting product (i.e., news packages, raw video footage, etc.) is made available to an array of CNN networks. Producers for each of CNN's news networks pick the reports they want for their shows from a "menu"

---

[3] CNN as early as 1982 was available in Japan and Australia.

[4] New entertainment networks created during this period include the Cartoon Network and Turner Network Television (TNT).

of stories, depending on their audience. Stephen Cassidy, senior international assignment editor and one of the key people responsible for deciding which news events get covered, compared the company's various news networks to a group of restaurants under common management, with the original "full-service" CNN channel offering "steak and potatoes":

> It's got talk shows. It's got interactive shows. It's got an hour-long format with long talk. We go to live events for a complete and total revelation of what's happening, whether it's an O.J. trial or a political convention.[5]

Headline News, on the other hand, is CNN's "fast-food restaurant," with quick updates on the top stories of the day repeated each half hour, while CNN en Español, the Spanish language service scheduled to go to 24 hours a day in 1997, represents

> our Mexican or Latin restaurant that appeals to the palate of people who speak Spanish and are interested in things in the world of Central and South America. . . . CNN International is our international café bistro. The special of the hour changes depending on what time it is. It is always prime-time somewhere.[6]

What makes CNN so efficient is that it can adapt the same news story to its ten different networks, keeping the per-story cost low in comparison to other networks, according to Cassidy:

> If Dan Rather sends a reporter to Timbuktu [who] spends $10,000 to send the story back to New York, they are going to put that story on the evening news tonight and it's going to play one time. Maybe CBS will take some pictures from that story and use them again tomorrow in their morning newscast. At the very most they will use their material once, twice, maybe three times maximum. If I send a reporter to Timbuktu to do a story for CNN . . . [the reporter] will send that report back . . . and any one of seven different networks . . . can use that material. Maybe within the course of 24 hours you might get 30 plays of the material. How much

---

[5] Stephen Cassidy (senior international assignment editor, CNN), from comments made to CNN's International Professional Program participants (September 1996).

[6] Ibid.

did the Dan Rather story cost? We know he spent $10,000. Let's say he played it twice. That story cost $5,000 a play. Let's say CNN spent $10,000 on the same story. We brought it here to Atlanta. We played it 30 times. How much does that story cost? It cost $300. Simple arithmetic.[7]

## Going Global

When Ted Turner ordered that the flag of the United Nations shoud fly at CNN's 1980 dedication ceremony (along with the flags of the United States and the state of Georgia), he gave a hint of his ambition to create an international news service. In the early years of CNN this goal was thwarted mostly by a lack of money and available satellite systems. Coincidently, about the time when Turner's news channels were beginning to make a profit in the U.S. market, major political changes around the world were creating unexpected and attractive opportunities in the global television business. State media monopolies around the world had begun to allow local competition. Alternative broadcast and cable stations were looking to offer a different mix of programming by providing entertainment fare as well as news imported by satellite. The rapid growth internationally of program channels and channel capacity created a market for non-local news, as audiences in India, Japan, Hong Kong, the Soviet Union, and South Africa found themselves dissatisfied with what they had been getting from state broadcasters. Entrepreneurs were beginning to realize that money could be made in marketing TV programs to Asia, Africa, Central and Eastern Europe, and Latin America.

The prospects for audience were huge and diverse. In even the poorest countries in these international markets, the segment of the population with disposable income was attracting advertising revenues. Even where infrastructures were weak and cash scarce, the perceived long-term potential was sufficient to attract international investors, and the U.S. and European media companies were all exploring the prospects. The growth of the global economy, coupled with CNN's readily available news programming,

---

[7] Ibid.

made the push to distribute CNN internationally an obvious business strategy for Turner. This strategy is now underway.

CNN now employs a satellite system that covers six continents, reaching some 210 countries and territories, with potential access to a half-billion people every day. Even in countries where CNN is unavailable to ordinary people—because of limited cable or satellite systems or because of political realities—CNN International has become the prevailing choice of viewers in hotel rooms, government ministry offices, and presidential palaces.[8]

On the newsgathering side, CNN's global growth has led to an increase in the number of international news bureaus to 21 and worldwide news staff to approximately 3000. Perhaps the most remarkable aspect of CNN's expansion is that it mostly occurred while American over-the-air networks were slashing budgets for non-U.S. bureaus. Carla Brooks Johnson gives a brief history of this development:

> As television technology grew in the 1960s and 1970s, the three U.S. Networks had taken the international lead in developing news bureaus in key locations throughout the world. They were joined by representatives from a few of the leading international broadcasters whose companies could afford such luxury. By and large, international coverage depended on transitory major events: wars, famines, the Olympics, and the like. In the 1980s, financial bad times hit hard for the "Big Three" in the United States, and similar broadcasters around the world. The networks lost about ten rating points in their nightly news, and each rating point cost them about $30 million. The networks cut foreign broadcast bureaus and news staffs and began to use the two global TV picture agencies (WTN and Visnews).[9]

The significance of CNN's global expansion became most evident during the Gulf War, when its wall-to-wall coverage not only produced the company's highest ratings, but led to much

---

[8] "Influential Europeans/Asians Study: Ad Sales Analysis," Center for International Strategy, Technology and Policy (Atlanta, GA: Georgia Institute of Technology, 1995).

[9] Carla Brooks Johnson, *Winning the Global TV News Game* (Boston: Focal Press, 1995): 57-58.

talk of a "CNN factor" (sometimes referred to as the "CNN effect"), whereby the network was thought to be inadvertantly shaping news events by virtue of its aggressive live television coverage.[10] CNN built much of its reputation as a credible source for international news on the basis of its on-the-spot reporting from such locales as Tiananmen Square in Beijing in May 1989, Baghdad under siege in January 1991, and the Parliament Building in Moscow in August 1991. These and numerous instances to follow also led to CNN's reputation as a news company whose very presence can shape the outcome of events it covers.

Despite the news company's aggressive news coverage, which can be distressful to the governments in power, CNN is now doing business in China, Baghdad, and Russia, and in 1997 has plans to open a bureau in Cuba.[11] According to Joe Hogan, senior vice president for network distribution at Turner International, broadcasters like China Central Television are valued customers of TBS and CNN. Although China has banned satellite reception of foreign programs for its citizens, Chinese officials have been willing to allow CCTV to receive Turner programs and selectively redistribute them within the country. According to Hogan,

> We fully understand that they do not want CNN International on a 24-hour basis to be distributed to every household in China. We respect that and will operate accordingly. . . . We don't have the view that we will rain down on a country via satellite television whether we are welcome or unwelcome. We will work with the powers that be, the state broadcasters, the ministers of communication, and we will abide by the rules of their country. . . . We do not want to force our products on them. We want them to look at our portfolio . . . and then go from there.[12]

---

[10] See Warren P. Strobel, *Late-Breaking Foreign Policy* (Washington, D.C.: United States Institute of Peace Studies, 1997), and his earlier article, "The CNN Effect," *American Journalism Review* 18 (May 1996): 33-37.

[11] No non-Cuban news organization has been allowed to operate a bureau in Cuba since 1969. In April 1982, CNN originated the first live American telecast from Cuba since 1958. After initially opposing CNN's initiative to open a Havana bureau, the Clinton administration backed the proposal.

[12] Joe Hogan (senior vice president for network distribution, Turner International), interview (August 1996).

And the Turner "portfolio" is selling well in China. Turner and CCTV have formed a number of commercial ventures. One of these is a deal that allows CNNI to be distributed to hotels throughout China. According to Hogan,

> It has been a very successful relationship on our behalf and very successful on their behalf. CNN is now in over 50,000 hotel rooms throughout China. . . . . It is a partnership that works well because both parties bring something that is absent in the other camp.[13]

The relationship with China may expand beyond news to include entertainment in the coming years, according to Hogan. Turner already distributes four hours a day of Cartoon Network programming to half a dozen provincial cable systems in China. "As we become a new company — Time Warner — with even more assets," Hogan said, "the relationship will come to include those areas as well."[14]

## Technologies of Distribution

One reason for the rapid rise of CNN has been the company's innovative use of communication technologies to reach its audience. At the center of this strategy are satellites, the miracle solution for Ted Turner's communication empire beginning with the national expansion of his Atlanta-based UHF television station to become Superstation WTBS in 1976. Satellites gave CNN a national audience in 1980, and have enabled Turner to be the first international broadcaster blanketing the globe using a mixture of Intelsat, Intersputnik, PanAmSat, and regional satellite signals when existing land-based systems could never have done the job.

Using satellites and a host of supportive terrestrial technologies, such as transportable satellite uplinks, lighter yet higher-quality cameras, and quick-turn-around digital editing machines, in addition to the standard fax and telephone, CNN's Atlanta-based staff maintain contact with international bureaus, correspondents in the field, and news sources everywhere — 24 hours a

---

[13] Ibid.

[14] Ibid.

day. Indeed, CNN's hallmark of live coverage would not be possible without satellites, which have helped the company get its live reports out of Libya, China, the Soviet Union, Iraq, Somalia, Bosnia, Peru, and other news hot spots around the world.

A family of technologies that will perhaps have an even greater impact on international operations of CNN—an impact not yet fully understood at this early stage of its development—is the Internet. As with satellite technologies, computer-based networks such as the Internet represent ways to overcome the physical limitations of one-way, limited-range broadcast signals. These technologies permit news to be exchanged quickly, leapfrogging political boundaries and border checkpoints silently and with ease, and they help to solve a host of logistic and economic problems as well. What opportunities the Internet will present for near-instantaneous access and coverage of the news is still being worked out. The fact that by the end of its first year of operation about a quarter of the "hits" on the CNN home page are from users outside the United States suggests that the Internet will be an important part of the network's continuing internationalization and global pressence.[15]

## Internationalizing the News

While "getting the news" is the company's stated priority, CNN managers have come to understand that *how* they go about getting the news and how they present it inevitably will affect the *perspective* of news. With this in mind, the company's managers—particularly for the international service—continually work to avoid the appearance of being a U.S.-oriented news network even while it is a U.S.-based company, according to CNN Senior Vice President Eason Jordan.

> A news network has to be based somewhere. This place works well for us. It is absolutely no shame in being based in the United States. You have to do it somewhere. If we were based somewhere else there would be questions about how being based there somehow skews our perspective. But it has to be stressed that most of the people who work for

---

[15] Scott Woelfel (vice president, CNN Interactive), interview (September 1996).

> CNN don't work in Atlanta. . . . It's hardly Atlanta alone that decides what's going to be on CNN. It's absolutely not Americans alone who decide what news is going to be presented and how that news is going to be presented. We have people here from all over the world who have real input into what's happening. It's not just a facade. This is the real thing.[16]

Jordan oversees the network's international news team of 250 full-time staff outside the U.S. and 25 assignment editors on CNN's international assignment desk. In that position, he has helped plan and coordinate CNN's coverage of the Gulf War, the U.S.-led interventions in Haiti, Somalia, Panama, and Grenada, the collapse of Communism in the Soviet Union and Eastern Europe, the war in the former Yugoslavia, the crackdown in Tiananmen Square, and the Korean nuclear dispute. One way that CNN has attempted to insure that its coverage of such events is not limited to an American view is to hire non-U.S. citizens to staff the desk. According to Jordan,

> There are some organizations who think, for instance, that an American network should have all American correspondents. There is great diversity in our presenting staff, in our reporting staff and in our behind the camera staff, and I think that is reflected in our programming and how we format our network.[17]

Another way to see to it that CNN has first chance at news wherever it happens, and that the news CNN offers is timely, relevant, and credible to an *international* audience, is to develop and maintain CNN's working relationships with television networks, news agencies, and broadcasting unions worldwide, all of which are a big part of Jordan's job. Even more important, perhaps, is Jordan's ability as a member of CNN's top inner circle—the Executive Committee—to help shape the company's strategic plan to internationalize the news network.

A key part of that plan involves partnerships with local broadcasters such as Wharf Cable in Hong Kong. Wharf has a license to redistribute the CNN service in its entirety 24 hours a day, with

---

[16] Eason Jordan (senior vice president, CNN), interview (August 1996).

[17] Ibid.

inserts of four half-hours per day of local news in English. Prior to teaming up with Wharf, CNN had a relationship with Asia TV Ltd., which aired 10 to 12 hours of CNN material daily. Satellite TV providers in various international locales are similarly licensed to deliver CNN directly to households, for which Turner collects a set amount per subscriber per month. Such an audience is not likely to tune in for long if the content is too American, or even too "local," for that matter, according to Joe Hogan;

> CNN is in daily pursuit of a balanced *global* newscast. Please keep in mind that this goes out and reaches a couple of hundred different countries and territories, so as they strive for that balance on a daily basis there is a high probability that they are not going to keep everybody happy all the time. If you try to achieve a Hong Kong-relevant broadcast, you will find that your broadcast will be less relevant for other countries. . . . What we try and do, what we feel is our strength, is in providing that global newscast [covering] the top stories of that particular day wherever those stories happen to be coming from. . . . We don't want to take on the task of competing with the local news broadcasters for that audience. It is inconceivable that we could do that given the fact that we are in 200 different countries. Within the last five years, with changes in our satellite feeds, we have tried to do a more regional broadcast. Two years ago we opened a CNN production center in Hong Kong that serves as a formal gathering place for materials the six bureaus collect on a daily basis. It also serves as a production point for some Asian programming to be done on a daily basis. So that is one example of our effort to regionalize a broadcast. Because that production center is located in Hong Kong, that doesn't mean it's news about Hong Kong. The Tokyo bureau feeds down, so does Thailand, Seoul, Manila, Jakarta. Hong Kong now serves as the source of the Asian business news program distributed on CNNI.[18]

But Eason Jordan noted that whatever success a news organization such as CNN has internationally depends less on specific partnership arrangements than on what such partnerships say about the company's "respect for the views of others," for all practical purposes the corporate mantra at CNN.

---

[18] Hogan, interview (August 1996). Emphasis added.

The example of such "respect" most often cited by CNN managers is CNN's *World Report* program, a controversial and little-understood undertaking of CNN founder Ted Turner, in which CNN airwaves are opened to broadcasters of all nations without editorial control. In October 1997, *World Report* marks its tenth anniversary of airing contributed reports from broadcast journalists around the world, none of whom is a CNN employee. The *World Report* staff in Atlanta assembles daily and weekly shows using contributed reports, editing them only if they exceed the time-limit of two-and-a-half-minutes. The program offers local broadcasters around the world the chance to be heard. And for Jordan and other key CNN managers, *World Report* offers the best evidence of the network's commitment to internationalize its news product;

> If there is any doubt about the respect we have for different cultures and different people, just look at the *World Report* program. We wouldn't do that program if we didn't have that perspective. . . . The *World Report* [has] gone a long way toward proving to people that we want to provide a number of perspectives on CNN and that we are truly a global news organization in every sense of the word.[19]

Similarly, Turner often uses *World Report* to underscore CNN's respect for other points of view, as noted in his November 1996 comments at the U.N.'s World Television Forum:

> What happens to cultures around the world as a result of the explosion of satellite television? How are we going to control this new development? . . . CNN was the first global network, and it was my idea. And I think we were kind of like the explorers back in the . . . 18th century. The first explorers, when they came from Europe in their ships, they were curious, and they were coming around to see what the rest of the world looked like. They didn't come with plans of conquest. And basically, they were welcomed everywhere they came. You know, when they came to the Americas, they were welcomed on the beach by the native peoples. . . . Then they went home and talked about all these new lands in Africa, India, China. You know, Marco Polo . . . . He was pretty benign. But then, after that, they said,

---

[19] Jordan, interview (August 1996).

"Ah, there's places here with the gold and people—we can make slaves out of the people. We can go get their gold and their trees and their animals, and we can get rich." And then came the conquerers, and colonialism. And I'd look at us as we were very benign. CNN was benign. We carried the *World Report*. We carried your reports. We listened. We only came in English, and we basically came through the local broadcasters. You could take whatever stories you wanted to, rebroadcast them. We were very benign.[20]

What CNN managers have come to understand and appreciate is how such unconventional Turner initiatives as *World Report*, the Goodwill Games, the environmentally-aware *Captain Planet* (a cartoon series) and other such gestures help CNN and its parent company TBS to think and act as a global entity, not just an American company with linkages abroad. These projects open doors not just for CNN's newsgatherers but also for TBS marketers, who sell their entertainment products around the world. According to Turner, such gestures have been important to CNN as the company seeks to better compete with global TV news providers such as the BBC, Rupert Murdoch's News Corp., and MSNBC. *World Report* in particular has been important to CNN as it seeks to define its broadcasting niche:

> The *World Report* came out of my head early on, because clearly, what we were, we couldn't be a local news channel, because we were limited to being an international and national news channel. So we had to really put some real emphasis on international and national. That's all we were. If all you have is a piano, you'd better learn to play the piano or learn to sing. If the only instrument you've got is a banjo, you learn to play the banjo. And I wanted to learn to play the international and national news game, so I had an international perspective from the very beginning.[21]

Companies that wish to duplicate CNN's global strategy, "CNN wannabes," as Eason Jordan has called them, will find CNN a hard act to follow. The principal reason is the unorthodoxy of Ted Turner.

---

[20] New York (22 November 1996).

[21] Turner, interview (December 1996).

THE THING THAT MADE ME THINK *internationally was my hobby with sailboat racing. I went all over the world racing sailboats. I started racing sailboats internationally in Mexico when I was in my twenties. I sailed across the ocean the first time to Europe in 1966. I raced all over the world — in Brazil, mostly in Europe and South America, and Australia and New Zealand. Unlike a tourist — tourists stay in the Hilton Hotel, they get on a tour bus, they get taken around by these tour guides. But when you go as an athlete you get to know the local people. You stay in their homes, you go to parties with them. I realized just how parochial most Americans are. We're such a big country and a wealthy country, and we think that the world — like the Romans did during the time of the Roman Empire — somehow circles around us, that we're the center of the universe. Of course, the Indians thought* they *were the center of the universe until the white man came. But Americans don't understand the world as they should. I learned the old saying, "When in Rome, do as the Romans do" when I went in these other countries. For instance, instead of going in a bar and bitching about the fact that there was no ice in the drink, I said, "Hey this is great," you know, "drinks without ice are okay." And beefing about the fact that there was no airconditioning, or that the local food isn't good because it's basically different. It's not that it's not good. Those people like that kind of food better than [our food]. So I developed through my yacht racing an international perspective that just suited me to a T.*

Ted Turner*
Vice Chairman, Time Warner Inc.

---

* Interview (December 1996).

# 2

# The Turner Paradox

*We're gonna take the news and put it on the satellite, and then
we're gonna beam it down into Russia, and we're gonna bring
world peace, and we're all gonna get rich in the process!*[1]

During much of his adult life, Ted Turner ridiculed news programming for its negativity and for its sensationalism.[2] This anti-
news view continued even after he created CNN, and probably
was a factor in his bid to buy CBS in 1985. At the time, Turner argued that owning the giant broadcast network would help him
reach many more eyeballs than TBS or CNN could, but more importantly, would teach the "arrogant" CBS broadcast network a
lesson for using the newsmagazine *60 Minutes* to attack such notable Americans as General William Westmoreland and former
President Jimmy Carter. CBS thwarted Turner's bid with an expensive buy-back of its own stock, which only reinforced Turner's
belief that

> the greatest enemies that America has ever had—posing a
> greater threat to our way of life than Nazi Germany or
> Tojo's Japan—are the three [U.S.] television networks and
> the people that run them, who are living amongst us and

---

[1] Ted Turner (vice chairman, Time Warner Inc.), to a group of young CNN jour-
nalists-in-training. Quoted in Hank Whittemore, *CNN: The Inside Story* (Boston:
Little, Brown and Company, 1990): 124.

[2] Peter Ross Range, "The Demons of Ted Turner," *Playboy* 30 (August 1983): 62.
In 1976, four years before creating CNN, Turner said: "I hate the news. News is
evil." Quoted in Tom Rosenstiel, "The Myth of CNN," *New Republic* 211 (22
August 1994): 27.

constantly tearing down everything that has made this country great.[3]

Turner's vocal complaints about the three giant U.S. broadcast networks and his budding international aspirations—particularly his friendly dealings with countries outside of U.S. political influence—were beginning to attract the attention of American media analysts.

> In the spring and summer of 1985, while bidding to buy CBS with $5.4 billion worth of junk bonds, Turner was also negotiating an agreement with the Soviet Union. On June 5 Robert Wussler, executive vice president of the Turner Broadcasting System and head of the Superstation, WTBS, announced that Turner's company had signed a two-year agreement with Gostelradio, the state-controlled Soviet radio and television network, to exchange news, entertainment, and sports programming.[4]

Turner's interest in things international, which resulted in part from trips to Cuba, the Soviet Union, and Africa, led the once politically conservative Turner to conclude that the "enemy"—as defined by the U.S. government—was not necessarily *his* enemy: "I happen to love everybody. Like Jesus, I've made my peace with the Soviets. They're not my enemies," Turner told the *New Republic* in a 1986 interview.[5] The transformation of Turner seemed real enough to disturb conservative journalists like Don Kowet, who was convinced by the mid-1980s that Turner had "absorbed too many ideas from his friends—including Castro—and now thinks of himself as a poor man's Armand Hammer."[6]

Turner had, indeed, discovered kindred spirits in those who argued that the western media flooded the airwaves, both domestic and international, with negative stories and cared about only a select group of societies and peoples, as reflected in their coverage.

---

[3] Adam Paul Weisman, "As Ted Turns," *New Republic* 195 (29 December 1986): 16.

[4] Ibid.

[5] Ibid.

[6] Ibid.

Nobody ever gave the Palestinians or the Arab side a voice. Not here in the United States anyway. They didn't have a voice. The most angry people in the world are those that don't get listened to. You can defuse so much anger by just listening to what the other [side says]. But if you don't give the man the chance to be heard, you know, like in court— you know, you go into court, you may not win your case, but at least the judge and jury listen to you.

We basically had a shutdown. In many instances the news media in this country were just as closed almost as they were in the government controlled countries. The news we got about Russia, or the Soviet Union, for the most part, was the stern unsmiling men sitting up there in the snow by Lenin's tomb, looking down on these thousands of soldiers marching through, and missiles and tanks and missile carriers. I saw that image a thousand times on television. I was terrified. All the little kids were terrified. They showed us how to get in bomb shelters. I mean, bomb shelters for nuclear bombs, are you kiddin'? We'd have all been dead. And we were being given this image of them, hardly ever did you see anything about ordinary Russian people, or interviews with them, that they had the same concerns about the situation as we did. They were doing the same thing with Russian television. They were showing us in our most unflattering light.[7]

The communication problem, as Turner saw it, extended beyond the Cold War; it was a bias on the part of those who collected and distributed the news.

I read about the non-aligned nations griping about the fact that the western news agencies controlled the flow of information around the world [giving] a very biased impression about the world. The only time that news about India gets into the international media is when there's something like Bhopal. That's absolutely true. It's outrageous.[8]

In early 1987, Turner had an idea about how to begin addressing the situation. Against the advice of his CNN management team, he decided to use the CNN channel as a way to respond to

---

the imbalance caused by American cultural imperialism. This was the origin of *World Report*.

> I was the one who said we were going to do it, and there was tremendous resistance. Everybody thought it was crazy. The braintrust of CNN, the little management group almost to a man thought it was outrageous that we would offer unedited time to Khadafi and Castro, the Russians, the Poles, the North Koreans. They just said, "You can't even think about doing that. No news organization in the history of the world has ever given up its airtime or its space on an absolutely unqualified basis to another news organization to give them access like that." And I said, "Well, everything we've done here is things that have never been done before, we're going to do that too. And I'm the boss and that's what I say." They had no choice. Like Walter Cronkite [said], "That's the way it is." That's the way it's going to be.[9]

## The *World Report* Initiative

Symbolically, if not completely, *World Report* opened the airwaves to broadcasters other than the elite of the world. In creating the program, Turner and his staff would establish a journalistic precedent—an on-going vehicle for airing multiple perspectives on local, regional, and world events.

> I basically was trying to use the *World Report* and CNN and my power as someone who had some influence in the media to make the world a little better place, to try and improve understanding and goodwill around the world.[10]

Turner gave the task of getting non-U.S. broadcast perspectives onto CNN to Burt Reinhart, the network's president. Reinhart, a consummate news manager in the American "hard-news" tradition, is reported to have sent form-letter invitations to broadcasters listed in the *World Radio-Television Handbook*.[11] Reinhart's invitation yielded no takers.

---

[9] Ibid.

[10] Ibid.

[11] Stuart Loory (former executive producer, *World Report*), interview (October 1996).

Never one to give up on a Big Idea, Turner turned to Stuart Loory, CNN's former Moscow bureau chief who had recently been transferred to the Washington, D.C., bureau.[12] Turner and Loory had often discussed global issues during Turner's visits to the Soviet Union in the mid-1980s, and Turner knew that Loory was likely to appreciate the idea:

> At the time I had a lot of different things going. I was trying to be one of these self-appointed goodwill ambassadors to end the Cold War. I didn't want to see the world toasted, which it was headed for. Nuclear annihilation had me greatly concerned, and I felt like there was something I could do about it, so I dutifully spent a lot of time in Russia with various initiatives, the Goodwill Games and all sorts of other ones, television exchanges, documentaries and discussion programs. So I got over there a lot, and Stu was our Moscow bureau chief, so I got to know him. And when his tour was up over there I had to have somebody to run it, and I [had] spent a lot of time with him . . . [and I] just basically discussed these sorts of things with Stuart and he shared that vision.[13]

Turner's visits to the Soviet Union also gave Loory a chance to get to know his boss better. He recalled one incident from the mid-1980s that helped him appreciate Turner's growing openness to new ways of thinking. On the last day of the visit, Loory, Turner, and a Soviet press officer were in a car driving through the streets of Moscow. From out of nowhere, Turner asked whether it was possible to become an honorary member of the Communist Party.

> Sergei [Gregoriev] turned around and said, "Yes, Ted, the Communist Party *does* have honorary memberships, but if you are thinking of an honorary membership for yourself, first of all, I am not sure that the Communist Party is really ready to accept you because they don't know you very well. And secondly I am not sure from a political point of view or a business point of view that you would be wise to even consider a honorary membership." And Ted said, "Well, I

---

12 The *Post-Soviet Media Law & Policy Newsletter* in September 1994 described Loory as the "respected, quasi-ambassador of Turner to the former Soviet Union." See: http://www.ctr.columbia.edu/vii/monroe/10two.html.

13 Turner, interview (December 1996).

guess maybe you are right." All of a sudden Sergei turned around and said, "But I will tell you what I can do. I am a member of the journalists union and I know I can get you an honorary membership at our journalists union." Ted got volubly and visibly excited and he said, "Absolutely not, I hate unions. We established CNN in Georgia because Georgia is a right-to-work state and we don't have to have unions there."[14]

Such exchanges helped Loory understand Turner's determination not to conform to the conventions of typical American broadcasters. When Turner invited Loory to Atlanta to create *World Report*, Loory understood that his task was to create a genuinely different kind of news program :

It was a very simple concept. All of the world's countries could tell the stories as they saw it. We would put them on the air, unedited, uncensored in any way. We would get the stories. They would pay for them. We would, in turn, give them free-of-charge the right to use the program, so that the program would have a worldwide audience.[15]

Loory very likely was the ideal choice to create *World Report*. He had an academic's critical outlook on the media system within which he and CNN operated, as well as credibility with journalists from non-western traditions. Peter Arnett, who took over as Moscow bureau chief when Loory returned to Washington in 1987, recalled that Loory and Turner were sufficiently popular among Soviet media officials to ease his own entrée into the Moscow reporting scene, but at a price:

The cordiality of our relationship with the Soviet authorities was not lost on the distrustful resident Western press corps. The correspondent I was replacing, Stuart Loory, was a respected professional of long Soviet experience whose credentials were unchallenged. But I began to hear CNN's objectivity questioned by suspicious colleagues.[16]

---

[14] Loory, interview (October 1996). Gregoriev was Mikhail Gorbachev's deputy press secretary.

[15] Ibid.

[16] Peter Arnett, *Live from the Battlefield* (New York: Simon & Schuster, 1994): 339.

The western media's reaction described by Arnett may have represented genuine concern over CNN's apparently cozy relationship with Soviet officials, or perhaps it was simply a case of sour grapes. After all, it was CNN President Tom Johnson who was in a position to offer his black Mont Blanc ballpoint to Mikhail S. Gorbachev when the Soviet president signed his own resignation in December 1991, an event described by *Atlanta Journal and Constitution* reporter Deborah Scroggins:

> Mr. Johnson flew to Moscow on Dec. 18 in the thick of fierce competition with ABC News to cover the first peaceful transfer of power in Soviet history. Holed up in the same hotel as Mr. Johnson, ABC's Ted Koppel had already obtained permission to film Mr. Gorbachev's last days in office. But when Mr. Johnson and CNN Vice President Stuart H. Loory visited the Soviet president on Dec. 20, he agreed to give them his first interview after his "decision," as Mr. Johnson delicately put it.
>
> After a false alarm on Christmas Eve, CNN was notified that Mr. Gorbachev planned to address the nation at 7 P.M. local time Christmas Day. Mr. Johnson and a 70-member CNN crew were rushed directly to the Kremlin's Green Room. Mr. Gorbachev . . . acknowledged the rise of CNN's clout even as his own waned. "You built your empire better than I built mine, but be sure to give enough power to your republics," the Soviet president joked.
>
> Mr. Johnson insists the inkless Soviet-made pen was not Mr. Gorbachev's final humiliation. But the symbolism evidently was not lost on the Soviet president. "American?" Mr. Gorbachev wryly inquired as Mr. Johnson handed him the Mont Blanc.[17]

## *World Report* Airs on CNN

Upon first seeing CNN *World Report*, viewers and even CNN insiders could be forgiven if they stared slack-jawed at their television screens. Journalists from Africa, South America, Europe, and

---

[17] Excerpted from Deborah Scroggins, "'We Did It! We Did It!' CNN Chief Says Scoop's The Thing, Not Famous Pen," *Atlanta Journal and Constitution* (29 December 1991): A6.

Asia were on "CNN air," giving firsthand accounts, often in heavily accented English, about events in their respective countries from their perspective, *whatever* it was. Starting that October, CNN televised up to three hours of contributors' reports each Sunday (or Monday, depending on the viewer's time zone). Each contributor had three minutes — later reduced to two and a half minutes — to tell the world what was important or interesting in his or her corner of the globe. "To paraphrase Andy Warhol," wrote the *International Herald Tribune*, "everyone gets to have his two and a half minutes" of uninterrupted air-time.[18] But what *would* the world's broadcasters say during their allotted time?

Media scholars familiar with the litany of complaints about western media from the developing world could have predicted that the stories submitted to CNN would be different from conventional American TV news in at least one important way: reporting by journalists from state-run broadcast organizations and from the developing world in general would be less critical and more "development" oriented.[19] That paradigm, which argues for minimizing *what's gone wrong* and stressing *what's going right*, emerged as a direct challenge to traditional western news values during the 1960s and '70s when the United Nations and UNESCO addressed inequities in global news flows.[20] Not surprisingly, calls for a New World Information Order to correct "imbalances" and the overwhelmingly negative demeanor of the news typically have been dismissed by western journalists as a ploy on the part of corrupt governments in the developing world to keep the critical western media in check. *World Report* gave the world's broadcasters a golden opportunity to do their *own* development journalism on CNN air. The question some scholars asked was, what would journalists from other parts of the world *do* with this opportunity?

---

[18] Sarah Veal, "CNN Passes Around the Mike," *International Herald Tribune* (11 May 1994): Finance section.

[19] Don Flournoy, "The Developing Story of Cable's International News Coverage," *Broadcasting* 114 (22 February 1988): 66; see also Flournoy, "A Global News Commentary," *Broadcasting* 115 (20 November 1989): 25.

[20] Probably the most frequently cited work in this area is Sean MacBride's *Many Voices, One World* (Paris: UNESCO, 1980).

# Nontraditional News

Several studies have examined the nature of news material submitted to *World Report* over the years. The premise of the content studies stems from a single, simple research question, articulated by Don Flournoy in 1992:

> After 20 years of complaining about how poorly the news collected by international agencies reflects life in their countries, broadcasters of the developing world now have a chance to put the record straight. On CNN's *World Report* they can correct whatever misimpressions and fill in whatever gaps they see by reporting events from their own perspective. Guaranteed a slot on an internationally distributed network, what do the local stations have to say?[21]

Flournoy's conclusions, and the conclusions of other scholars who have examined *World Report* over the course of 10 years, are that—at least as far as topics are concerned—"the news seen on *World Report* is the same old news of the world."[22] In other words, *World Report* news reflects the conventional news definitions of its many conventional contributing journalists, who focus mostly on domestic and international politics, economics and business news, and news of military and defense actions that is the basis for international news nearly everywhere.[23] *World Report* does,

---

[21] Don Flournoy, *CNN World Report: Ted Turner's International News Coup* (Luton, U.K.: John Libbey and Company, Ltd., 1992): 37.

[22] Ibid., 96.

[23] The first content analysis of *World Report*, which examined the first year's contributions, was completed in 1989. Rachada Kongkeo, "A Content Analysis of CNN *World Report*: Development News from Non-Western Perspectives 1987-1988," Masters thesis, E. W. Scripps School of Journalism (Athens, OH: Ohio University, 1989). Other early studies included Rani Dilawari, Robert Stewart, and Don Flournoy, "Development Orientation of Domestic and International News on CNN *World Report*," *Gazette* 47 (1991): 121-137; Don Flournoy and Chuck Ganzert, "An Analysis of CNN's Weekly *World Report* Program," *Journalism Quarterly* 69 (Spring 1992): 188-194; Chun-il Park, Rani Dilawari, and Don Flournoy, "Development Orientation of Domestic and International News on the CNN *World Report*," Research Monograph, Institute for Telecommunications Studies (Athens, OH: Ohio University, 1992); and Lisa McClean and Robert Stewart, "The Caribbean Story on CNN *World Report*: In Search of 'Development News,'" *Gazette* 55 (1995): 55-67. For a rundown of Sunday *World Report* stories,

however, include a greater percentage of news topics focusing on environment and ecology, arts and culture, science, health, and social services than appear elsewhere.[24] This could easily be a function of the freedom that contributing reporters are given when they submit stories to *World Report*, without interference from assignment editors and producers. In the case of *World Report*, contributors are *encouraged* to bring their own perspective to bear on the report. This, in fact, is the most significant journalistic difference between the practice of western broadcast journalism and that of *World Report*, according to Flournoy;

> A greater number of international news stories are being told from the perspective of those closest to the events, sometimes by those affected personally, as with the reports from Lithuanian TV (its station surrounded by Soviet paratroopers) and JRT-Croatia (its cities being bombed.)[25]

Stuart Loory, the founding editor of *World Report*, similarly characterized the stories submitted to the program as "distinctly nontraditional interpretations" of the news.[26] Perhaps that's what the *Chicago Tribune* had in mind when it described a 1990 report submitted by Cubavision:

> The three-minute TV story on German reunification opened with malnourished Africans ambling along a dusty road. Then it bashed the United States, the Soviet Union and Western Europe for "forgetting about the Third World" by focusing on European matters. Clearly, the report by Cuba's

---

see the *World Report* Archives Web site, maintained by Texas Tech University, at: http:// www.ttu.edu/~cnnarch/.

[24] A 1997 study shows "that foreign relations news and the news under arts/culture category continued to be the types of stories most frequently aired on the CNN *World Report* during the 1992-1996 period." Sangchul Lee and Ece Algan, "CNN World Report: A Five Year Analysis," Research Monograph, Institute for Telecommunications Studies (Athens, OH: Ohio University, 1997).

[25] Flournoy, 96.

[26] Stuart Loory, "News from the Global Village," *Gannett Center Journal* 3 (Fall 1989): 172.

state-run television network was a different slant on a hot issue.[27]

But even stories that don't confront U.S. or European authorities so directly provide the global audience with a refreshing look at the world, a look that still makes Ted Turner smile:

> On the *World Report* we got a report from one African nation, and they had the band out at the airport, and they were welcoming the president of Liberia or some other country. So you saw an African leader get off the plane being greeted by another African leader, the flags of both countries there, countries you've never heard of or hardly ever see, and *they're* meetin' with each other. I mean, light bulb goes on: "Hey, there are other meetings going on in the world besides us and them."[28]

Content analyses of *World Report* also support what any extended viewing of the program likely will reveal: journalism that focuses less on negativity and more on solutions to the world's problems, a form of journalism not unlike what Davis "Buzz" Merritt,[29] Jay Rosen,[30] Arthur Charity,[31] and James Fallows[32] have called "public journalism." A study by Park and colleagues examined 566 *World Report* stories submitted by a total of 106 broadcast news organizations during 1990-91. The study showed remarkable similarities between the contributions of the so-called North and South countries. In presentation of domestic news (news concerning the internal issues of a country), both the developed and the developing countries focused more on development news than on non-development news. Yet, both the developed and the

---

[27] James Warren, "CNN Show Offers a Motley, Manipulated Look at World," *Chicago Tribune* (4 March 1990): 1.

[28] Turner, interview (December 1996).

[29] *Public Journalism & Public Life: Why Telling the News Is Not Enough* (Hillsdale, N.J.: Erlbaum, 1995).

[30] *Getting the Connections Right: Public Journalism and the Troubles in the Press* (New York: Twentieth Century Fund, 1996).

[31] *Doing Public Journalism* (New York: Guilford Press, 1995).

[32] *Breaking the News: How the Media Undermine American Democracy* (New York: Pantheon Books, 1996).

developing countries oriented their coverage more toward non-development news in what they offered as international news (news involving two or more nations), according to Park, who concludes that

> If CNN *World Report* is an example of the ideal (New World Information Order) newscast—in which countries are free to present their own news from their own perspective—we may be seeing a news trend in the use of development journalism by both the developed and the developing countries. Namely, development news is as likely to come from the North as well as the South, the affluent as well as the poorer nations of the world.[33]

*World Report*, then, is more an "anthology of TV from many sources, some of which is crude and may be gathered in ways that are different from what Westerners are accustomed to," according to media scholar Everette Dennis.[34] The program's limited (but thought to be loyal) following in the United States may reflect the fact that Americans are less accustomed to watching what may seem like oddball stories, contrasting sharply with the broadcast news that fills the American networks' international news hole.[35] Despite the presence of solid, groundbreaking journalism on *World Report*, it is the quirky *World Report* story about "dancing birds in Kuala Lumpur," as one staffer put it, that seems to stick out like a sore thumb, even providing a form of journalistic comic relief for the program's critics. The *Chicago Tribune* mused in 1990 about a *World Report* viewing experience that encompassed stories about

> poignant medical and economic travails in Africa; bizarre ethnic conflicts on exotic islands that viewers may have to

---

[33] Park, et al., 11.

[34] Quoted in Jane Hall, "CNN's *World Report* Celebrates Its Fifth Anniversary with a Two-Hour Retrospective on Sunday," *Los Angeles Times* (24 October 1992): F1.

[35] Studies of the U.S. broadcast networks show that they typically devote only about 20 percent of their nightly news programs to international news, no matter how big or small the international news story. See James B. Weaver, Christopher J. Porter, and Margaret E. Evens, "Patterns In Foreign News Coverage on U.S. Network Television: A 10-Year Analysis," *Journalism Quarterly* 66 (Summer 1984): 356-363.

consult an atlas to locate; a Swedish view of tumult in Romania; penis transplants in Thailand; the suicide of an 86-year-old Osakan after Japanese real-estate speculators pressured him to sell his house; and a ho-hum fair of religious artifacts in Bolivia.[36]

On the other hand, observed the *Record* as far back as 1988, *World Report* offers a strange kind of

proof that life goes on in the village, even in the absence of death and destruction. . . . At the end of 90 minutes, the world seems a less horrible, more human, infinitely larger place than the vale of geopolitical tears presented nightly by the networks. And yet, it feels more intimate, more like the village we keep hearing about.[37]

Not surprisingly, this is much like what Turner says he set out to create when he first envisioned the program:

The *World Report* was to let the whole world be heard. To open up the whole world. . . . Our information before the *World Report*, before CNN, was like the spokes of the wheel, where everything was from the United States out and the United States back. That's all the information we ever got. And now all of a sudden, with the *World Report*, you were seeing what was going on, like brain cells, numerous brain cells instead of one. There were all these other countries that are connected too. But we had [had] no view of that.[38]

From Turner, proponents of a New Information Order received a sympathetic—almost enthusiastic—hearing. If Turner hoped to "save the planet and save the human race," he needed diverse views on CNN to offer viewers different perspectives on the news, and "positive" stories to counterbalance the negative ones that filled the more traditional newscasts at CNN. He could count on *World Report* contributors, many of them less hung up on American standards of objectivity, to help find ways to humanize distant cultures for viewers who heretofore had received only stereotypical images. But could he count on his own staff?

---

[36] Warren, 1.

[37] Greg Dawson, "Closer Terms as the World Turns," *The Record* (24 February 1988): E22.

[38] Turner, interview (December 1996).

## The Insider View

Not surprisingly, the CNN staff didn't buy it. Airing reports from broadcasters with journalistic agendas and abilities that fell short of what the public had come to expect of CNN was not a universal "hit" at the network, recalls Ralph Wenge, longtime *World Report* anchor and now executive producer for the program.

> A lot of people [at CNN] didn't like what they saw, didn't like the idea of this program. When Ted first came up with the idea, there were a lot of people in this company who fought it.[39]

One can imagine, as did *Newsweek* media critic Jonathan Alter, in a 1990 report, that anxiety levels rose even higher when contributed reports occasionally made their way onto conventional CNN:

> With portions of the *World Report* now abutting pieces by CNN correspondents abroad, where does "perspective" end and blur begin? These juxtapositions create the possibility of confusion and represent an acknowledgment that there are few consistent standards for what appears as news on CNN.[40]

The *Chicago Tribune* in 1990 concluded that *World Report*'s view of reality could leave "American TV anchors, reporters and editors wincing over its unabashed polemics."[41] Indeed, many of those wincing anchors, reporters, and editors worked at CNN and clung to the gilded "CNN Standard" for objective journalism despite Turner's effort to force a broader definition of news. Bob Furnad, executive vice president for CNN and the person who must oversee everything that goes onto CNN air, long has fretted over the blurring lines that may cause viewers to confuse CNN work and *World Report* work. Even at the ten-year mark, some CNN journalists still see the program as stretching the boundaries of journalism to the breaking point, leaving former *World Report* staffers like Kim Norgaard, now working on the international as-

---

[39] Wenge (executive producer, *World Report*), interview (September 1996).

[40] Jonathan Alter, "Ted's Global Village," *Newsweek* 115 (11 June 1990): 48.

[41] Warren, 1.

signment desk, trying to explain the concept of the program to colleagues.

> One sometimes does hear negative criticism (here at CNN and elsewhere), but maybe it is because they are too set on how news should be done and don't really understand the concept of *World Report*. I had a conversation with a CNN producer the other day who said: what is this crap? I explained how I look at the show not just as these other voices but representing something of the anarchy of the event itself. [*World Report*] is more like the incident where there is no particular order to it and you can say what you want and these voices can be heard whether you like them or not. That is the whole point.[42]

*Newsweek*'s Alter conceded the point, noting that "For the discerning viewer, the *World Report* provides terrific perspective, not just on global news but on the whole nature of propaganda."[43] CNN's new vice president in charge of news production on CNN's international channel (CNNI), Chris Cramer, agreed that the program offered the audience something different, something to react to:

> There would be very few people in the building and very few people who watch the program who from time to time don't wince, but that's not the point. That absolutely is not the point. The point is, if the audience wins, good. It means this program is getting a response, and it *does* get a response.[44]

Even as it marks its tenth anniversary, *World Report*'s critics within and without CNN still fail at times to comprehend the story within the story on *World Report*, according to Cramer;

> There's an intellectual exercise in watching *World Report*, which is the extent to which you can select those correspondents and reporters from around the globe who you can feel them sort of shaking the chains in their reporting. And then there are the ones who are perfectly happy to be in chains—

---

[42] Kim Norgaard (assignment editor, CNN International Desk), interview (October 1996).

[43] Ibid.

[44] Chris Cramer (vice president, CNN International), interview (September 1996).

that's a bad word—but in the suit. Perfectly happy to be there, and are proud about being there. And what's great are the different types of reports you get, and the extent to which journalists are either fighting against the country or the institution they are working in, or are comfortable with it.[45]

## Doing Business Doing Good

During his years at the BBC before becoming managing editor for CNN International in 1995, Cramer kept tabs on *World Report* in part because of a "sort of skepticism from conventional broadcasters about exactly what Turner and CNN were up to."[46]

What Turner was up to, it would seem, was relatively simple, according to CNN International's Eason Jordan;

A lot of criticism from people who didn't really know any better thought that CNN was some sort of imperialistic force out to dominate the world in some sense. Ted's reason for launching *World Report* was to allow journalists from all over the world to see CNN from the inside out and see that we are sincere and honest and impartial in everything we do.[47]

The reasons why CNN would host a no-cash exchange of news that included the poorest stations as well as some of the most affluent broadcast enterprises of the world—airing all their stories as perspectives without editorial comment or control—are complex. The most obvious reason was that TBS chairman Ted Turner wanted, indeed *willed* it to happen. In the TBS organization, that reason alone is sufficient.

I was really pretty highly motivated. But at the bottom of it I thought it was going to be good for business too. I didn't know it was going to be good for business. I didn't know if

---

[45] Ibid.

[46] Ibid.

[47] Eason Jordan (senior vice president, CNN), interview (August 1996).

we were going to be able to make real money off it. I mean, nobody'd ever done it before.[48]

In *Covering the World: International Television News Services*, a commissioned work for the Twentieth Century Fund, Lewis Friedland noted how Turner's "internationalism was coupled with a shrewd understanding of a changing international news market, well before any of his competitors." Friedland gave Turner credit for understanding that the international news market would be limited to several major organizations, that the horizon for becoming a "player" was short, and that penetration of all world markets was a prerequisite for success.

> Almost from its inception, CNN founder Ted Turner has had an international vision for his network that reflects his personal ambition as well as his growing interest in world ecology and nuclear disarmament. In a 1993 address to the National Academy of Television Arts and Sciences, Turner said he was more concerned with contributing to "salvation of life on earth" than making money on CNN's international ventures. And in 1982 he told *Time*: "I want to start dealing with issues like disarmament, pollution, soil erosion, population control, alternative energy sources." Turner's interest in global ecology and disarmament drove CNN toward Moscow and Beijing.[49]

The Turner Paradox—the belief that social responsibility and making money can go hand in hand—is one of the *central* Turner strategies in the international news business. What may not be obvious to CNN viewers is that *World Report*, a decade after its debut, remains the most significant and enduring example of Ted Turner's direct intervention into his network's news programming. Even more significant is how Turner and CNN managers have deliberately and methodically used the *World Report* to make CNN more international—in its news gathering, distribution, on-air presentation, perspective, and appeal.

---

[48] Turner, interview (December 1996).

[49] Lewis A. Friedland, *Covering The World: International Television News Services* (New York: Twentieth Century Fund, 1992): 22.

I THINK THAT THE CNN *WORLD REPORT is the coolest thing we do. I think it's better than CNN itself. Ted Turner thought of CNN and that was a great idea. And then he thought of the* World Report, *and that was an even better idea. That's my opinion. . . . The criticism was,* "You big fat white Western guys there in the United States, you got your news networks, you're out there telling the world what the world is, what's going on. And here we are, the developing countries, we don't have a lot of technology, we don't have a lot of money. We never get a chance to portray ourselves in front of the world, so how do we ever get an even break?" Ted said, "OK, come on down. I'm going to invite you up to my electronic podium a couple times a day, couple times a week, and I'm going to put you on TV and you can say anything you want. I'm not going to edit it, I'm not going to have anything to do with the content, you decide what you want to put on TV and we'll just introduce it. We'll say, "Ladies and gentlemen, here's the* World Report. *Here's the stuff that people sent in. Look at this." You get a report in from Pyongyang, people are up there sending in stories about the great rice harvest, you know, and they go completely against what you might be hearing someplace else, but, who knows? That's their side of the story.*

Stephen Cassidy\*
Senior International Assignment Editor, CNN

---

\* Excerpted from comments made to CNN's International Professional Program participants (September 1996).

# 3

# The *World Report* Factor

*If Marshall McLuhan's global village exists, its capital is the CNN headquarters in Atlanta.*[1]

*World Report* was not just an act of do-goodism, but an innovation that the company badly needed. CNN was expanding internationally. It needed to build bridges to every country in the world to gain access to content and to market its products. It needed to change its own corporate and organizational culture to insure that its staff had the professional and social skills to operate in an international environment.

The practice of putting non-standard news sources onto CNN air began before *World Report*, according to Henry Schuster, senior executive producer for CNN and one of the original producers of CNN *World Report*. Because the company was working to create a global newsgathering operation on a shoestring budget, CNN sought out stories from broadcasters in places where it had no bureaus or readily available correspondents. During the Communist crackdown in Poland, CNN excerpted Polish TV newscasts, and during the Falklands War, material from Argentine television.

*World Report* is the institutionalization of the practice of putting nontraditional perspectives onto CNN air. That practice has rewarded CNN with some high-profile, if controversial, scoops, according to Turner;

---

[1] Joshua Hammer, "Triumphant Ted Turner, the Swashbuckling Media Visionary Brightened Our Hopes for a Global Village," *Playboy* 37 (January 1990): 76.

√ We never would have been allowed to stay in Iraq during the Iraqi war if it hadn't been for *World Report*. We've gotten a lot of access as a result of our making a real effort to having people from other countries and other news organizations feel comfortable about us. We've got a lot of access to world leaders and so forth, and then, allowed to be behind the lines and allowed to stay in circumstances where other news organizations weren't allowed to. Partly that was the case that we'd been allowed because so many world leaders were watching us when there's a conflict anywhere in the world, or anything controversial, where people, where leaders need to get their point across. Like Saddam Hussein did. At least we gave him some access during that war. We gave the Iraqis access that they otherwise would not have gotten if CNN wasn't there, because basically we believe that everyone has a right to be heard.[2]

Schuster underscored the advantage *World Report* gave CNN in gaining access to Iraq, and the impact that airing Iraqi perspectives had in proving that CNN did, indeed, practice an open-door policy;

*World Report* helped us reach a lot of places and win a lot of colleagues — I won't say friends — in some diverse places. We had a relationship with folks at Iraqi television before the Persian Gulf War. We were very actively trying to get them to contribute to *World Report*. We were getting regular contributions from Iran; we wanted to get contributions from Iraq. They had been here [in Atlanta] during the early *World Report* contributor conferences. That gave us some degree of respect and entrée. Even now, when CNN is a lot larger, to some we may seem something of a monolith, these people know that they can still get their pieces on, get their side of the story told, get the story told the way they want it told.[3]

---

[2] Ted Turner (vice chairman, Time Warner Inc.), interview (December 1996). Peter Arnett, who remained in Baghdad for CNN during the Gulf War, discounted the importance of *World Report* per se, but he told the authors that Iraqi authorities allowed CNN to stay in Iraq because of the network's willingness to give Iraqi President Saddam Hussein access to CNN air. Peter Arnett, interview (January 1992).

[3] Henry Schuster (senior executive producer, CNN), interview (August 1996).

Tom Johnson, president and CEO of the CNN news group, has argued that this effort to embrace such a wide array of perspectives is unprecedented:

> I know of no other news organization, no other company in the information business, that makes such an effort to reach out. Especially to reach out to those media people who continue to be influenced by their governments. We *know* they cannot freely talk about politics, but they are able to cover areas like sports or areas like culture or features. . . . Isn't it better to have a partial look into these really highly diverse nations of the world and give them an opportunity to convey information about so much that is not political?[4]

According to *Newsweek* media critic Jonathan Alter,[5] *World Report* accomplishes what Turner hoped it would

> provide television viewers around the world with the opportunity to see other countries as they see themselves. CNN *World Report* gives the world's broadcasters a global forum from which to report the news as they see it, to the rest of the world. The *World Report* staff does not exercise editorial control over content and airs all contributions. Participating broadcasters gain worldwide exposure in CNN and CNNI's shared audience of more than 170 million pay TV households. In exchange for submitting reports, contributors receive rights free of charge to rebroadcast material from CNN *World Report* as they wish.[6]

When Stuart Loory created *World Report* in 1987, he had hoped that contributors' work would be highly visible and integrated into CNN's *conventional* news programs;

> I always thought the CNN *World Report* contributors [were] the beginning of CNN worldwide news service. My thought there was that in addition to the reports that all of these people were contributing, basically free of charge as far as CNN was concerned, from time to time [they could] be asked by CNN to do special reports for which they would be paid.

---

[4] Tom Johnson (CEO/president, CNN), interview (December 1996).

[5] Jonathan Alter, "Ted's Global Village," *Newsweek* 115 (11 June 1990): 48.

[6] Excerpted from the *World Report* homepage. See: http://cnn.com/CNN/Programs/WorldReport/index.html (December 1996).

[These reports] would appear not in the *World Report*, but would appear in other CNN programs.[7]

Loory's original vision has yet to be realized, for only rarely does a *World Report* news package get into the "run-of-network" pool from which every CNN producer can draw stories. But that should not be taken as a measure of the program's impact on conventional CNN news programs. Its primary value to the network lies in the relationships with other broadcasters, according to Eli Flournoy, an assignment editor on the CNN International Desk and a former intern in the *World Report* unit. These contacts can, at times, lead directly to expanded coverage of international events that otherwise would get little play.

A dramatic example of this was CNN's unprecedented coverage of the Hajj, the annual Muslim pilgrimage to Mecca in Saudi Arabia, in 1996. CNN received permission from the Saudi government to downlink the live camera pictures of millions of Muslim pilgrims in Mecca praying in unison. On the phone with CNN to provide live commentary was Abdul Abu-Khudair, a reporter/anchor for Saudi TV's Channel 2 and a contributor to *World Report*. CNN executives had debated whether Abu-Khudair should be put on CNN air, knowing he likely would not mention possible negative incidents such as expected demonstration from the Iranians. However, CNN news managers understood that Saudi television had a unique ability to cover this story, which is inextricably linked to the nation's religion and culture. Saudi television had an ongoing relationship with CNN through *World Report*, and the feed service — which is similar to the Vatican's television coverage of the Pope at mass — provided the only way CNN viewers could *see* the event.

CNN's acceptance and airing of Saudi TV's coverage illustrates how *World Report* relationships influenced the extent to which CNN was able to cover an aspect of international society. And similar stories abound, according to Flournoy. A search of the CNN video archives for file footage of North Korean President Kim Il-Sung produced no pictures to accompany the CNN reports

---

[7] Stuart Loory (former executive producer, *World Report*), interview (October 1996).

about his death. Flournoy knew that North Korea had been an intermittent contributor to *World Report*. He found footage of Kim Il-Sung in the separately maintained *World Report* library and used it as the visual component of the story that was aired on CNN's domestic and international networks. Kim Norgaard, a former *World Report* assignment editor now working on the CNN International Desk, had a similar experience:

> There was a plane crash in some Norwegian islands up north which are mainly populated by Russians. But we had no video. I wondered if Norway had ever filed a *World Report* piece from there. So I ran up to *World Report*, found a tape and we had file pictures we could use to show people what the islands looked like.

The *South China Morning Post* in 1993 noted that China Central Television contributed a 90-second story to *World Report* on the welfare of three prominent Tiananmen activists, Wang Juntao, Chen Ziming, and Wang Dan, including heretofore unseen video of the three dissidents.[8]

*World Report* also has helped CNN provide news coverage of less remote locales as well. Researchers at Ohio University, under a grant from the Canadian government, examined media images of Canada in U.S. newspapers and magazines, as well as on the U.S. network television news programs. The findings, published in *Media Images of Canada*,[9] demonstrate what many Canadians have suspected all along: their neighbors to the south rarely learn about Canada through the U.S. media:

> One would not suspect from the coverage that Canada is the leading trading partner of the U.S. Recent major issues such as separatism and the environment simply have not gotten adequate coverage in the U.S. media. The study also points out that Japan gets far more coverage than Canada—four times as much in some media. This applies to trade and

---

[8] Daphne Nickson, "Reunions for Dissidents," *South China Morning Post* (15 February 1993): 8.

[9] Don Flournoy, Debra Mason, Robert Nanney, and Guido Stempel III, "Canadian Images of Canada: U.S. Media Coverage of Canadian Issues and U.S. Awareness of Those Issues," *The Ohio Journalism Monograph Series* , E. W. Scripps School of Journalism (Athens, OH: Ohio University, 1992).

economic coverage, and the average U.S. media user can only assume that trade with Japan must be far more important and far greater than our trade with Canada.[10]

CNN provided database printouts of Canadian stories appearing on the network during 1990 and 1991, and made available video copies of CNN's *PrimeTime* (8 P.M. Eastern time) newscast.[11] Not surprisingly, the researchers discovered that the 24-hour news network's coverage of Canada far exceeded that of any U.S. broadcast network. What was surprising to both the researchers and CNN news managers was that the vast majority of the Canadian stories were collected by Canadian journalists and aired on the *World Report* program. Without the *World Report* stories contributed by Canadian journalists, CNN's coverage of Canada was barely average, with 25 reports collected and produced by CNN newsgatherers in 1990 — only 16 of which appeared in its *PrimeTime* newscast. But when *World Report* contributions were included in the study, CNN's coverage of Canada jumped to a total of 366 news items aired, an average of about one story per day — far exceeding what the other broadcast media had to offer.

News reports contributed to *World Report* occasionally make their way into other CNN programs — usually either in the form of stock video that is unavailable from other video services, or as part of other feature programs, such as *CNN Newsroom*, aimed at students and teachers. But this potential never has been fully realized, partly by design. *World Report* packages *should* be seen as distinct from other CNN reporting. That is why they are aired on a special program with clarifying lead-ins that tell viewers that these are perspectives, according to Will King, in charge of CNN's International Desk.

The distinction is partly a function of *World Report*'s place within the institutional structure of CNN; it is not a part of CNN International per se but rather of CNN's Features department. Yet *World Report* is a daily part of CNNI's programming schedule — to

---

[10] Ibid.

[11] When the study was done, the Vanderbilt Network News Archives included only ABC, CBS, and NBC newscasts. CNN newscasts now are available through the archive.

a greater extent than on CNN's U.S. service. The Sunday program takes up three hours of CNN International's weekend feed, and four hours of the domestic weekend programming.[12] In each of these programming slots, *World Report* material is contained within the parameters of the *World Report* program. In King's view, having *World Report's* contributors become regular CNN or CNNI newsgathering agents would violate the true intent of *World Report*. Practical problems have occurred when *World Report* contributors and CNN reporters sought the same interview to put on CNN air. An example was recalled former *World Report* executive producer Nancy Peckenham;

> Egypt TV would tell the president they are requesting an interview for CNN and, true, it *was* on CNN, but that was Egyptian TV. So when [CNN reporters] came in to make a request for the president, they would say, "Oh you have already talked to so and so." It gave confusion in the field sometimes when understandably people working for CNN would be confused by the difference between *World Report* and CNN reports.[13]

Despite the potential for confusion, King has seen *World Report* contributors as important assets for the International Desk at CNN, mainly because they can help assignment editors become aware of — and get access to — important stories;

> *World Report* contacts are beneficial to us in breaking news. These are people who know us. Have an allegiance to us. Typically they are willing to provide guidance to a breaking story. A lead to follow up on. To do a phone report for us.[14]

He cited the example of a border dispute in Cyprus in which several people were killed. *World Report* contributors from both north and south Cyprus did an important job of telling viewers about the situation from their unique point of view, King said. Tom Johnson

---

[12] On CNNI, one of the two shows is a two-hour program; the other show repeats the first hour of the two-hour program. On CNN's U.S. service, the two-hour show is televised twice, for a total of four hours.

[13] Nancy Peckenham (former executive producer, *World Report*), interview (November 1996).

[14] Will King (managing editor, CNN International Desk), interview (December 1996).

frequently cites ways the Turner organization has benefitted from these arrangements. Through *World Report*, CNN was able to give these local news stations the means to tell their side of the story to a larger audience, to the benefit of that station *and* CNN.

> *World Report* has enabled CNN to establish trust throughout the world. It has enabled CNN to build relationships with broadcasters in all the many countries which we serve and it has clearly enabled the broadcasters of the world to have their reports seen by a global audience uncensored, so that their voices, their cultures, their economies, the special news of their individual cities and areas can be better understood by people around the planet.[15]

The result of these relationships is the expansion of CNN's "family," according to Johnson.

> By that I mean, while not every one of the [contributing] stations . . . perhaps operates by the exact same standards of independence that can be practiced in countries with greater press freedoms, it has enabled CNN to broaden its reach.[16]

## International Professional Program

*World Report* contributors, including those from both sides of the longstanding Cyprus conflict, have spent time at CNN Center in Atlanta, meeting with the CNN staff firsthand, either through the contributors' conferences or via the company's International Professional Program, which four times each year offers *World Report* contributors the opportunity to participate in an intensive six weeks of training. Since the IPP started in 1989, more than 200 journalists, media producers and managers from more than 100 news organizations have participated, interacting with the highest levels of CNN management and being assigned to work with CNN departments of their choice.

"[The IPP] was another brainchild of Ted's," according to Lou Curles, director of international protocol for TBS/CNN. Curles— fondly referred to as "Mama Lou" by many of the program's

---

[15] Johnson, interview (December 1996).

[16] Ibid.

participants—joined CNN during *World Report's* first year (1987) and has organized most of the IPP sessions over the years;

> We started that first session in October, 1989, starting a twelve-week program, which we later reduced to six weeks. We now do four sessions a year and have managed about 25 of these since that time. . . . We have tried to select someone from each corner of the earth and to have someone represent each country at least once a year. The IPP participants must have at least three years of experience. It is *not* an internship program. It is for seasoned journalists who are *World Report* contributors to come here to improve their skills.[17]

IPP sessions take up 24 weeks out of each year—meaning that for nearly one out of every two weeks during the year CNN is engaged in providing training for contributors. Participants spend time discussing journalism with CNN news executives from every part of the company, including senior managers. Such interactions can make a powerful impact, according to one IPP participant, Simone Duarte from TV Globo:

> Tom Johnson sat at a table with us and said: "Tell me what you think of CNN," and he really listened. And I think the owner of Globo, I never have been with him. In this way I was very impressed that Ted Turner was sitting with me, or Tom Johnson. Not because it was Ted Turner and Jane Fonda or Tom Johnson, but because they are listening to me.[18]

IPP participants also can work shifts on the assignment desk, or contribute to CNN's product in their own unique way during their stay in Atlanta. One such instance was recalled by *World Report* producer Susan Winé:

> Nigeria's MST sent us a story about body carvings, and the writer at the time, Karen Leggett, who was this NPR reporter freelancing for us, was, like, "Nigerian body carvings?" And I said, "Oh, you need more information for the anchor intro? It just so happens that I know a Nigerian with body carvings who's sitting at the desk right around the corner. Her name is Biola [Odunewu]. Let me introduce you." And so Karen

---

[17] Lou Curles (director of international protocol, TBS/CNN), interview (December 1996).

[18] Simone Duarte (foreign editor, TV Globo), interview (October 1996).

Leggett and Biola from Nigeria were able to sit down and talk about the importance of body carvings.[19]

Such exchanges create powerful bonds at the institutional and personal level, according to CNN president and chief executive officer Tom Johnson;

There are many graduates of the training programs that CNN has run since 1989 . . . [who] are today in the management and the leadership of television stations throughout the world. There are even some of the *World Report* contributors who [now] are part of the CNN staff.[20]

For newsgathering, Johnson noted that *World Report* has

expanded the eyes and ears of CNN in places where we otherwise could not have reached with our own reporters. And I think maybe the most important part is that it has enriched our programming by giving contributors and IPP staffers, as part of this whole family, the opportunity to convey to us what they are all about, to convey to our editors, producers, and staff their individual stories in a way that we will have a better understanding [of where they come from] than we would have had had we sent Western-educated personnel into these areas and asked them to do research.[21]

The ties that bind CNN to the IPP participants grow strong over the six-week period they spend together in Atlanta, according to Curles;

In my layman's language, I like to say that it has made a global family. As with any family, you stay together, you talk together. Be it to help your station or to help CNN. As you have heard [people say] many times, when we need information from somewhere, it is very easy to pick up the phone and call a *World Report* contributor or a former participant in the IPP.[22]

---

[19] Susan Winé (producer, *World Report*), interview (September 1996).

[20] Johnson, interview (December 1996).

[21] Ibid.

[22] Curles, interview (December 1996).

## *World Report* Contributors Conference

One of the most important opportunities for *World Report* contributors to interact with company executives is at the annual contributors conferences, held at CNN Center for five days each spring. These conferences reinforce the mission of CNN *World Report* by providing a forum for international journalists to communicate with each other as well as with CNN management and staff. They also bring to Atlanta — and to CNN — a legion of international television journalists as well as newsmakers to seek their audience; the impact on CNN proper of this invasion of internationally-minded journalism is profound, according to Stuart Loory;

> I think the beginning of the impact [of *World Report* on CNN] came with the conferences and the start of the conference. I was always pretty confident if the conferences continued, that they were really going to add luster to CNN and Turner Broadcasting.[23]

The conference schedule typically features panel discussions and presentations by world leaders. In effect, the scope of the conference transforms it into a *media event,* in which *World Report* contributors become central players through their question and answer exchanges with newsmakers, all of which is made available on tape by CNN for broadcasters to use back home.

The 1996 conference, attended by nearly 300 journalists and executives from news organizations in more than 70 countries and territories, was typical of the six conferences that preceded it, in the fact that it aimed to help contributing broadcasters broaden their understanding of issues ranging from the Cold War to race/gender biases in the media. Invited guests included two Nobel laureates (Joseph Rothblat, 1995 Peace Prize winner for his Pugwash conferences on Science and World Affairs, and Wole Soyinka, 1986 Literature Prize as a prominent black African playwright in exile); several world leaders (U.N. Secretary General Boutros Boutros-Ghali; Chairman of the Central Committee of

---

[23] Loory, interview (October 1996). Loory: "The thing that I had in mind in doing those conferences . . . was the *New York Herald Tribune* Forum, which I attended in my youth."

Russia's Communist Party Gennady Zuganov via satellite; Prime Minister of Israel Shimon Peres via satellite; former Mali head of state Amandou Toumani Toure; former U.S. President Jimmy Carter; American social and political figure Reverend Jesse Jackson; Co-Chairman of the Atlanta Committee for the Olympic Games Andrew Young); and other expert speakers and panelists (*In Search of Excellence* author Tom Peters; Ohio University Cold War historian John Gaddis; CNN's Beijing bureau chief Andrea Koppel; its Jerusalem bureau chief, Walter Rogers; international correspondent Christiane Amanpour; Charlayne Hunter-Gault; talk show host Larry King; and anchors Jonathan Mann, Bernard Shaw, and Judy Woodruff).

But the contributors conferences are not comprised solely of high-minded seminars and soul-stirring speeches. At the request of conference attendees at previous conferences, as well as of the contributors who are informally consulted during the planning stage, conference organizers have begun including hands-on workshops led by CNN professionals.[24] Even more evident at the conference in recent years is the presence at the conference of the Turner International Sales staff, which began holding its annual planning meetings in Atlanta to coincide with the spring contributors conferences. As one contributor described it,

> You get introduced to TBS news service for example. [The Turner company] goes beyond CNN. Then you get to know one of the CNN reporters you have seen on TV and you shake hands with him and you get in touch with him [so] that would make you more open to have CNN in your service.[25]

An unstated theme of the conference, as with previous *World Report* contributors conferences, was CNN's pervasive role as the

---

[24] CNN Voice and Dialect Consultant Judith Sullivan and CNN International Anchor Sonia Ruseler conducted a voice workshop; CNN Executive Producer David Bernknopf offered "tips on how to improve scripts and overcome overwriting." CNN Photographer Roger Herr demonstrated video techniques "to capture more powerful images and record more compelling sound." (Conference brochure, 1996)

[25] Fernando Jauregui (reporter/producer, CMT-TV Venezuela), interview (November 1996).

world's media "host" for global affairs, a role noted by the *Houston Chronicle*'s TV critic, Ann Hodges, following the 1994 conference, which included an appearance by U.S. President Bill Clinton on the *Global Forum* program that CNN hosted from the Carter Center in Atlanta;

> It's a measure of the global clout of Turner's first international news service that not only Clinton is here, but [also] Israeli Prime Minister Yitzhak Rabin and PLO Chairman Yasser Arafat also appeared together via satellite for a similar town meeting. Today, town meeting stars will be President F. W. de Klerk and President-elect Nelson Mandela, together on satellite from South Africa.[26]

Madeleine Albright, then U.S. Ambassador to the United Nations and one of the speakers at the 1994 Contributors Conference, compared it to "a town hall of the global village";

> I haven't seen this many people from foreign countries in one room since the last U.N. general assembly. A convention for news junkies from around the world. By week's end, I expect all our problems to be solved.[27]

Given the lineup of speakers willing to attend, the gathering is a publicity windfall for CNN. And it is compelling evidence that CNN's internationalization agenda helps build relationships, puts names and faces with telephone voices and contributed stories, and insures that international affiliates and *World Report* contributors see CNN as accessible.[28] For CNNI's vice president, Chris Cramer, who joined the network in 1996 after a long career with the BBC, the conference revealed an underlying truth;

> Part of the *World Report*, which is the unspoken part of it, is the extent to which it enhances our profile internationally, and gathers and develops for us around the [world] tens of thousands of journalists who have great affection for CNN, and my god, have we reaped the benefits of that over the years, as you will observe [at the conferences]. I've only been

---

[26] Ann Hodges, "Clinton to Take a Grilling from the World," *Houston Chronicle* (3 May 1994): 4.

[27] Ibid.

[28] Winé, interview (September, 1996).

to one and I couldn't believe the level of good will . . . the level of excitement among very senior journalistic managers who had actually come to Atlanta for *World Report*. I found that really quite emotional. And I'm not talking about young reporters who reported for Ralph [Wenge]. I mean very senior broadcast executives who found themselves in this kind of building. It was an . . . extraordinary experience. A rather expensive revival meeting.[29]

Leading the revival meeting every year is Ted Turner himself, who devotes considerable attention to the conference and its attendees. Turner attends panel sessions and many of the conference social events, is available to anyone who wants to talk to him or have a photograph taken, and always offers the contributors his own brand of public speaking that entertains while admonishing his audience to do a better job of saving the earth:

We're in the position to save the planet and save the human race. We're all communicators for peace, saving the environment and rights for women. We can release the military [funding] to deal with family planning [and the] environment.[30]

Media star and wife Jane Fonda also attends conference events and even serves as occasional panel moderator. *World Report* contributors' access to Turner and top CNN executives during the annual contributors conference probably is more than most CNN employees have during the year. The effect can be humbling, according to Fernando Jauregui, the *World Report* contributor from CMT-TV Venezuela.

When you see such a high-level manager staying with you in one of the poorest segments of CNN, you know that despite how much money they manage or [do] not manage, they value the segment, because they are giving a whole week of their time. That's a guy that might make a fortune with one decision in one hour, but he stays most of the time with you for five days. That's why I think . . . that not only helps to

---

[29] Chris Cramer (vice president, CNN International), interview (September 1996).

[30] Turner's comments at the 1994 Contributors Conference in Atlanta, quoted in Ann Hodges, "It's Unanimous: CNN a Major Player; Broadcasters from Around World Agree on Network's Clout," *Houston Chronicle* (7 May 1994): 6.

introduce CNN products, but also makes you understand or value the work you are doing for the *World Report*, because *they* value it.[31]

And the payoff for CNN is real, according to Turner.

What goes around comes around. If you put out evil, evil's going to come back to you. The Bible says, what you sow is what you're going to reap. And the *World Report* and the IPP program—that was my idea too—[helped us] because there was a great resistance to us out there in the world. [They were saying] "What's going on here? We don't want satellite television coming from the United States." People didn't know me. They didn't know what we were up to. They suspected the worst, that this was going to be some kind of imperialism.[32]

Equally important, according to Johnson, is the impact the conferences can have on CNN personnel.

I think our staff came away [from the *World Report* conference] with a better understanding of some of the issues in that very complicated Balkan area once we brought to the conference representatives of the Serbs, representatives of the Croats, so that we could meet them firsthand. I think it was important having President Clinton and Christiane Amanpour debate the issue. With Christiane in Sarajevo and President Clinton here in Atlanta, and having Madeleine Albright addressing the group, I think all of us came away with a better understanding of the complexities, the difficulties of the issues that face all sides, that face the peace negotiators.[33]

---

31 Jauregui, interview (November 1996).

32 Turner, interview (December 1996).

33 Johnson, interview (December 1996). During the *Global Forum* program with U.S. President Bill Clinton, Amanpour, who appeared live by satellite from Sarajevo, suggested in pointed questions to Clinton that his administration's policy on Bosnia had been inconsistent. Amanpour: "Do you not think that the constant flip-flop of your administration on the issue of Bosnia sets a very dangerous precedent and would lead people . . . to take you less seriously than you would like to be taken?" Clinton: "No, but speeches like that may make them take me less seriously than I'd like to be taken. There have been no constant flip-flops, Madam." "*Global Forum* with President Clinton," The Carter Center's Day Chapel, Atlanta (3 May 1994).

The influence of *World Report* extends beyond simple, if important, "awareness" issues. CNN Senior Producer Henry Schuster
contends that CNN and CNN International have steadily adopted
an approach to news writing that he and his former colleagues on
the *World Report* staff pioneered — that is, avoiding automatic
judgments that an American-centric news staff would tend to
make. He said viewers can recognize that attention to detail and
cultural sensitivity when they listen to the writing on CNN or notice the program content on CNN International.

> In a sense, we were trying to blaze that trail. When I came to
> [*World Report*], you would hear people write: "Sri Lanka, a
> country the size of Rhode Island. . . ." For the audience we
> were aiming at there was just no frame of reference to know
> where Rhode Island was. We viewed our audience as inter-
> national. We had a U.S. audience. We realized that a great
> deal of our U.S. audience, at least from the mail that we were
> getting, was ethnically based. By that, I mean you had people
> watching who had a connection to Serbia, or they were In-
> dian or Pakistani. These people were watching, so we wanted
> a newscast where the writing was free of U.S.-based meta-
> phors, things which would have been incomprehensible to an
> international audience. For example, we started using the
> metric system. We had to refer to things in kilograms pri-
> marily. If someone made reference in their piece to an
> amount of currency, we would make reference to that cur-
> rency and the U.S. dollar. We developed our own writing
> style — Siobhan Darrow (now an international correspon-
> dent), Lori Waffenschmidt (now producer of weekend fea-
> tures) and myself. I wouldn't call it a value-free writing style.
> I don't think that is ever possible. But we did make a con-
> scious effort to not let the news reflect our biases.[34]

While such influences are more obvious to past and present
*World Report* staffers than to others at CNN, *World Report* Executive
Producer Ralph Wenge said he now is confident that "at least
[senior management pays] attention to what we're doing now, because they realize we play a relevant role."[35] And certainly, high
profile managers such as Tom Johnson, Eason Jordan, and Chris

---

[34] Schuster, interview (August 1996).

[35] Ralph Wenge (executive producer, *World Report*), interview (September 1996).

Cramer readily acknowledge the increasing relevance to CNN of *World Report*. As the program adapts to the CNN environment in which it operates, it gradually has taken on some of the more western characteristics of conventional CNN news, making it more likely to appeal to the conventional television news crowd working behind the scenes at CNN. Wenge, who pushed for going live even prior to being named executive producer in 1995 (following a long association with the program as one of its main anchors), argued that taking the program to a live format would keep it from being preempted whenever a major news story broke.

> CNN *World Report* is different, but it *is* a news program, and we've become more hard news. We still take the features, we still take the light stories, we still talk about the cultures of the different countries, but it is also a hard news vehicle from [the contributors'] perspectives. Not from the perspectives of the correspondents that CNN sends around the world. But from the journalists who actually live in those regions of the world where the stories are taking place. And I think, yes, it gives it a much more strategic location in the whole network. The rest of the network does tend to look at us a lot more differently now. They take us more seriously, and that's something I've been striving for ever since I've started this, [and] I think we *are* gaining more respect. *Now* we have other parts of the company saying, "Gee, can we use a certain story? Can we use one of your contributors to enhance the story we're covering, because we don't have a bureau there?" It's part of the growing process of the whole program.[36]

Ironically, while the influence of CNN's live news format is increasingly evident on *World Report*, the evolution of *World Report* into something more CNN-like will likely, in the end, assure that its influence on the network will deepen. What may not have been well understood, even by Ted Turner, was how *World Report* would help internationalize company personnel, both in terms of recruiting new employees and in terms of retooling the existing staff. *World Report* provided the network with a needed global outlook by challenging conventional (i.e., "American") ways of doing news and forcing a reorientation of the network's own culture, thereby sharpening the cross-cultural competencies of

---

[36] Ibid.

Turner's staff. Thus, what was thought to be an overly-generous concession to on-air diversity at CNN and a contribution to a two-way flow of news internationally — which in fact it was — has also helped CNN reposition itself to more effectively operate in a global market.

Scott Herron, a *World Report* producer, originally joined CNN after a long career in newspapers — including the largest newspaper in Hungary — because of the network's international outlook;

> Whenever I would be traveling abroad and would come back I would always be shocked by network news, by how parochial it is, how almost stridently right-wing. Once I get settled in it doesn't sound that way. But when I come back to the country my immediate thought is how [nationalistic it is].[37]

After working as a writer for CNN International for five years, Herron was lured to the *World Report* in part because of *World Report's* fundamentally different approach to news.

In the years since joining CNN in 1991, Herron has noted the effect on the people *World Report* brings under the network's umbrella:

> If you just look at this building, it's filled with people from all over the world. We just had an intern, a Russian. She had some sort of fellowship, and she came down here to intern. She just got hired as a VJ [video journalist]. Another guy from Curacao just got hired as a VJ. So those people are all coming into our organization. Eventually those people are going to be producers and editors, and it's going to change the culturalization of the show. Now, obviously they've come into this culture; it's a two-way street. That's how educational programs enter into foreign policy, because you want them to start thinking *your* way. But as those people are absorbed into the workplace here, they will make a difference [in the workplace itself].[38]

*World Report* colleagues are perhaps the best examples of this phenomenon, according to Herron. Octavia Nasr has served both as a

---

[37] Scott Herron (producer, *World Report*), interview (August 1996).

[38] Ibid.

*World Report* assignment editor and as anchor: "Here's someone who speaks French, Arabic and English. She's Lebanese." *World Report* assignment editor Andrew Henstock is Scottish with a Ph.D. in French, while assignment editor Claudia Chang speaks Chinese and comes from German-Chinese ancestry. Debra Daugherty, an assignment editor and anchor, lived in Brazil and Panama and speaks Portuguese and Spanish. According to Daugherty, "many of us come to the network as regionalists. At World Report, we evolve into internationalists."[39]

*World Report's* effect on CNN personnel extends beyond the *World Report* unit, however, according to Schuster;

> Imagine Ralitsa [Vassileva] who comes from Bulgaria anchoring not only *World Report* but a weekly newscast from CNN International. TV is often about anchors themselves. That puts a very different face on the international newscast. With a mix of staff, global and local hires in the late '80s and early '90s, people like Maria Ressa, Ashis Ray, we were doing some in Korea as well. Ted felt, for the same reasons he had about *World Report*, that they were plugged into the country, that they would report without the biases of an outsider.[40]

Members of the Atlanta-based *World Report* staff who have moved on to other parts of the news company no doubt take with them both a familiarity with the program and a greater understanding of its basic mission. As Norgaard noted, his *World Report* experience brings another dimension to his work on CNN's International Desk;

> It is always helpful now that I am on the International Desk to know there are people in these countries whom I can call at the TV station, names of those who can help with breaking news or whom I can interview on the phone. It all depends on how open their media laws are. Some (contributors) would like to be helpful for background but don't want to be on the air. But they will point me in the right direction.[41]

---

[39] Debra Daugherty (assignment editor, *World Report*), interview (February 1997).

[40] Schuster, interview (August 1996).

[41] Kim Norgaard (assignment editor, CNN International Desk), interview (October 1996).

Some notable former staff members who moved into other positions within CNN include executive producers Stuart Loory (to become a CNN vice president specializing in international projects), Donna Mastrangelo (to become executive producer for CNN International and later to join the network's *Milinium* project) and Nancy Peckenham (to become executive producer for CNN's New York bureau), as well as a host of former producers (e.g., Henry Schuster, Lori Waffenschmidt, and Janet Kolodzy[42]), assignment editors, writers, and tape editors who have gone on to other CNN positions.

## The *World Report* Paradox

Claudia Chang, who joined CNN *World Report* as an assignment editor in January 1996, has as her primary responsibility Asian contributors. One of the countries in her "beat" is the People's Republic of China, where *World Report* is helping CNN gain access to developing world markets, according to Chang;

> More and more contributors are from stations being established in regional China, away from the CCTV bureaus. Shanghai, one of the financial capitals in China, now has five or six local stations. Some of these are developing client relationships with Turner International. They are also broadcasting parts of CNN or CNN International on their stations. Most of these stations have English news programs, in addition to their regular Chinese broadcasts. When I first moved to China, I thought these English language programs were for the benefit of Westerners or foreigners living in China. Then I learned after a time that they are for Chinese people to practice their English.
>
> As more and more of the regional stations participate in the IPP program, they come back with a widened idea of what kind of television people around the world are exposed to. Many of the contributors I work with were initially surprised about the concept of *World Report*. It just seemed

---

[42] Schuster is senior executive producer at CNNI; Waffenschmidt is executive producer for CNN's environmental/ science unit, and Kolodzy is a producer for CNNI.

fantastic to them that there is no censoring going on, no editorial control.

They say, "Oh, so you don't censor anything?" More and more people are learning about *World Report* in China. CCTV takes two hours of *World Report* every week and turns it around and broadcasts it out on the local stations. CCTV is now like many of our contributors who rebroadcast *World Report* on their own station. Right now, there are about 15 million people who live in Beijing alone. As more and more people move to the city and as more and more improve their standard of economic living, the TV is one of the first things people are going to buy. The number who have direct access to CNN in their homes is small. Some see it in hotels. But the closer you get to Hong Kong, the more able Chinese citizens are in gaining access to CNN directly from the satellite.[43]

But while the potential economic windfall from relationships created through *World Report* is very attractive to CNN, Johnson argued that the primary motive for creating *World Report* and the IPP training program is noncommercial;

I know some people search for the commercial motive here, but this is done primarily as a public service of Ted Turner and Turner Broadcasting. It was not designed to build affiliates. It was not designed to produce new subscribers. It was not designed to produce increased advertising. . . . We really are careful not to try to commercialize it. I think if we were to, it would lose much of its value. If I say it has helped us to improve our content, helped us to improve our understanding, that is all true. But we don't use *World Report* as some covert way to attract more business to CNN. . . . It was really designed as a public service to enable communications to flow between all these nations.[44]

---

[43] Claudia Chang (assignment editor, *World Report*), interview (August, 1996).

[44] Johnson, interview (December 1996). When the staff of the International Desk interacts with journalists from these 100 stations, they consider it a network–affiliate interaction. When the *World Report* staff in Atlanta interacts with those same journalists, they consider it to be a *World Report*–contributor interaction. This explains, at least in part, why the International Desk and the *World Report* staff do not always give equal credit to the contributions of *World Report* within the context of the network's overall programming/ newsgathering efforts.

Nevertheless, the practical benefits to the network of having CNN-friendly journalists in an organization such as China Central Television are obvious even to Johnson.

> As I look at the composition of the International Desk and our international people, we have set up feeds directly from CCTV into CNN where it would be a *World Report* or IPP person that is assisting us with a press conference. It is people out there who know us, respect us, trust us and if they have a choice in assisting CNN or one of the other networks, where they don't have this type of relationship, I think we get an added advantage from that.[45]

That these contacts represent every imaginable type of news organization in the world *has* helped the network achieve an international outlook, according to Norgaard, an international assignment editor;

> It adds a lot more voices to those we have on the International Desk. It is nice in that it makes us look less like a purely Western media organization.[46]

The newsgathering benefits of *World Report* were obvious to CNN—and others—almost from the beginning. Just three years after Stuart Loory created *World Report*, one media critic already was calling the program "a linchpin of Turner's renegade vision and strategy for the decade":

> By allowing nations to say virtually whatever they want, Turner has become the manager of a journalistic array of disparate products and quality, and thus has forged ties that give CNN advantages in a competitive media marketplace.[47]

*World Report* already has won for CNN—and its parent company TBS—enormous international favor during its first decade, earning for it distinct economic, practical, and competitive advantages as well as good will.

---

[45] Ibid.

[46] Norgaard, interview (October 1996).

[47] James Warren, "CNN Show Offers a Motley, Manipulated Look at World," *Chicago Tribune* (4 March 1990): 1

## Ten Years Later

Despite evidence that *World Report* increasingly flirts with conventionality, the fundamental premise of the program seems intact at the ten-year mark: CNN televises virtually all contributed material—without censoring or editing the report—provided it is less than two and a half minutes. And whatever concerns *World Report* may raise for the news purists at the network, the program has the backing of Ted Turner and key news executives, if for no other reason than it opens doors that might otherwise be closed to an American news organization. The bottom line, according to CNN Vice President Eason Jordan, is that *World Report's* contribution to CNN is partly what makes the network different from other broadcast news organizations:

> If you are going to think in a traditional sense, the easiest thing to do is not to do it at all. Clearly, there were some risks associated with (*World Report*), but Ted being the visionary that he is, saw beyond the traditional thinking, saw this could be a huge advantage for CNN in many ways that would off-set any concern traditionalists might have about whether it is appropriate to air this type of material on CNN. [*World Report*] is always done and will be done in a way that will make it absolutely clear to viewers that the content in the *World Report* program and the content from *World Report* contributors that would air as part of CNN is simply sharing the perspective of a broadcaster. As long as you present everything properly and set up the pieces properly there is absolutely no reason to be concerned about journalistic credibility. Now, if you muddy the waters and for some reason don't do that, of course there is greater cause for concern. Without a doubt this program has been a huge success for CNN.[48]

CNN's international news managers see *World Report* as far more than an idle experiment or intellectual exercise. The program offers CNN a vital forum within which to exchange ideas with journalists who otherwise "would have been yelling imperialism and colonialism not so long ago," as Richard Shaffer, who studies

---

[48] Eason Jordan (senior vice president, CNN), interview (August 1996).

international media, has noted.[49] These journalists now are *part* of CNN, bringing in news from around the world and transforming the news mix on the network.

---

[49] Sarah Veal, "CNN Passes Around the Mike," *International Herald Tribune* (11 May 1994): Finance section.

IN AN AGE OF ALMOST INSTANT *communication, where, if there is slaughter in Rwanda and Burundi, it's on television within minutes – the same in Somalia – it forces the foreign policy-makers (the president, the secretary of state, all of us) to react sometimes more quickly than wisdom would prefer. Sometimes we ought to be thinking about some of these issues, but particularly because of television, and particularly because of this very network we're on – CNN – the speed with which these things are reported sort of demands an answer from the government, from policy-makers, almost instantaneously, and that's not always good. But whether it's good, bad, or indifferent, we're stuck with it. And my view of it is that we have had to learn to live with it.*

Lawrence Eagleberger[*]
Former U.S. Secretary of State

[*] Excerpted from comments on CNNI's *Q&A* (24 January 1997).

# 4

# Gathering & Producing International News

*I've heard it denied by U.S. government spokespeople, but I'd say the way CNN reports the news as it happens puts pressure on governments. They have always had to react to major international events, but now they have to do it faster. They can't fall behind the CNN curve. Everyone else has seen the event on CNN, so everyone wants to know, "What's the government's position?"*[1]

During his stint in Baghdad covering the Persian Gulf War for CNN, Peter Arnett became one of the world's most visible reporters. Ten years earlier, when Arnett joined CNN, most Americans had no idea what the brash, aggressive reporter from New Zealand looked like, even though his coverage of the Vietnam War for the Associated Press in the 1960s and '70s was equally controversial—certainly in the eyes of the administration of U.S. President Lyndon Johnson. The difference between the two reporting experiences was that Arnett's reporting from Baghdad was accomplished using *live* television.

Since his famous Baghdad assignment, Arnett has divided his time between field reporting for CNN, writing a book,[2] and giving lectures. During a conference on media coverage of war,[3]

---

[1] Bruce Jacobs (producer, CNN International), interview (January 1997).

[2] Peter Arnett, *Live from the Battlefield* (New York: Simon & Schuster, 1994).

[3] "Making War and Keeping Peace: What Should Television Report?" The Baker Peace Studies Program, Ohio University, Athens, Ohio (26-27 April 1996).

Arnett compared the U.S. government's reactions to his reporting of the conflicts in Vietnam and Iraq. "In Vietnam [the U.S.] could bomb the breadth and length of the country at will and have briefings on the daily body counts in the field without concern for public reprisals back home."[4] By the time of the Persian Gulf War—and no doubt partly as a result of the U.S. death toll in Vietnam—"there was fear of the public learning that a single U.S. soldier might be killed."

The accelerated speed of coverage is believed by some to accentuate the impact that journalism has on policy-making. Prior to television—and particularly *live* television—information came by the diplomatic pouch or by secure telephonic communications. Arnett pointed out that information in the post–Cold War world now comes *live* from the crisis zone via independent media, unfiltered by governments or their military debriefers. It now is part of the television reporter's responsibility, whether in Haiti or Lebanon or Bosnia, to interview *all* players on location and report directly to the viewing public—including governments and their diplomats who themselves rely on the visual media as a principal source of information about what is happening in the world.

International news coverage is reshaping government-press relations and giving the media an even greater role in forming public opinion. During the Vietnam War, President Johnson convinced most of the U.S. press corps that coverage of the war should remain limited as a matter of national interest. It was on this basis, Arnett noted, that President Johnson could justify having the Federal Bureau of Investigation develop a file on him "to see if it could find something it could use against me as a reporter."[5]

CNN's predisposition toward live coverage has raised the spectre of a "CNN Factor" that would cause governments and other international bodies to make decisions based on immediate

---

[4] Peter Arnett, "Peace, War and Global Communication." An Elizabeth Evans Baker Lecture, Ohio University, Athens, Ohio (26 April 1996).

[5] Ibid.

media reporting and resulting public reaction to events.[6] Now, instead of trying to hide information from the media, a government is just as likely to use the CNN cameras as a "way of telegraphing its position around the world."[7] Writing in the *Harvard International Journal of Press/Politics*, U.S. State Department spokesman Nicholas Burns described how such coverage has made CNN a player in diplomatic circles:

> CNN has become so pervasive in its worldwide coverage that it is sometimes an actor itself in global politics. Take a breaking news story, such as a coup or natural disaster in any part of the world, and chances are CNN will have a reporter there to cover it within minutes. CNN is so good that it regularly beats our own embassies and consulates to stories. Its broad coverage of events day in and day out is the best way for diplomats and citizens to follow world events.

> The CNN phenomenon is so widespread that it has revolutionized the way diplomacy is conducted in the modern world. First, CNN makes it easier for diplomats around the world to follow what is happening. I turn on CNN International at 7:00 A.M. in my office and keep it on throughout the day. Its jingles and theme music provide the backdrop in government offices and palaces from Santiago to Seoul.[8]

Working as a writer and producer for CNNI since 1993, Bruce Jacobs said he believes he has been witness to a "quickening pace of international relations" as a result of CNN's immediate coverage.

> CNN is a primary source of information. When we're live with breaking news, you can't get the information any faster. We're there as it happens. We're there as 100,000 Rwandan refugees walk down the roads out of Zaire. We're there as hostages walk out of the ambassador's residence in Lima, Peru. We're there as the Gulf War breaks out. If reporters see something on CNN in the morning, they may

---

[6] Warren P. Strobel challenges the existence of such an effect in his article, "The CNN Effect," *American Journalism Review* 18 (May 1996): 33.

[7] Arnett, lecture (26 April 1996).

[8] "Talking to the World about American Foreign Policy," *Harvard International Journal of Press/Politics* 1 (Fall 1996): 13.

ask the U.S. State Department spokesman about it that afternoon. One would hope Nicholas Burns would have an answer or position on that matter by then.

Do the pictures from places like Zaire or Bosnia or Rwanda affect government policies around the world? I've heard a lot of government denials about the effects of CNN pictures on policy. I've heard the U.S. State Department say the government had a policy on a crisis well before Christiane Amanpour arrived on the scene. It can't be stated as a fact, but in my opinion, watching how governments react to news events and pictures, I'd have to say those things do affect policy.[9]

But being used as a common carrier for messages of government puts an enormous responsibility on the media, including CNN. CNN Executive Vice President Bob Furnad has been responsible for the network's landmark coverage of many live events, which has helped build CNN's reputation for being first in breaking news. While helping define "live coverage" as part of CNN's niche in the news business, Furnad said he sees a downside to some of the new capabilities to go live:

I don't think that live availability always creates a positive situation. In years when there were no satellite transmissions, when there was a crisis and government leaders made statements, it could be days before an affected government would respond. They would take the time to review all their alternatives, to craft and give their response. They had the time to work with it, to examine it from all sides and make sure that what they were doing was what they wanted to do and that it was sending the right message. Today when the president of any country can go on national or international television and make a statement about another country, about another world leader, because of this live availability, because of what we and other news media do, there is an unspoken pressure on the person on the receiving end to respond quickly. So what have you lost? You have lost the time for measured thought. You have lost the time for a full debate within the inner circles. You have lost the time for a crafted response. So what hap-

[9] Jacobs, interview (January 1997). Jacobs was with CNN Headline News from 1991 until joining CNNI in 1993.

pens is a self-imposed quick response that might not be the right response. The availability of this live international media is positive in terms of the citizens of the world knowing what is happening to them and to others, but it isn't necessarily a positive [development].[10]

Furnad acknowledged that world political leaders are fast learning how to use the live media to their own advantage. Politicians *everywhere* seem to have figured out how to get the exposure they want through live television news coverage almost whenever they want it, sometimes with a surreal effect. Jacobs remembered one such occurrence in April 1996;

> One weekend . . . there was heavy fighting in Liberia between forces loyal to Charles Taylor and those of Roosevelt Johnson. Monrovia was being torn apart by the violence and the looting that followed. Taylor had accused Johnson of murder and, in attempting to arrest Johnson, the fighting had broken out.
>
> At the height of the battles, Taylor called CNN and we put him on the air for an interview, and he described the situation from his point of view. He had talked to us before on the phone, so we had a beeper graphic already prepared for him.
>
> About an hour later, Roosevelt Johnson called. Apparently, he was watching Taylor [on CNN] and called to dispute his assertions and gave his point of view of the fighting and the murder charge against him. He said the charge was bogus and politically motivated.
>
> Taylor called back later, and we put him on the air again. The assignment editor on the International Desk told me when he talked to Taylor and his people, he could hear CNN International was on in the background.
>
> We told the desk to try to get them both on the phone at the same time, and, if possible, we could hold a debate/negotiating session on our air. However, we were not able to get both of them on the line together.[11]

---

[10] Bob Furnad (executive vice president, CNN), interview with Paolo Ghilardi (December 1996).

[11] Jacobs, interview (January 1997).

Furnad related an instance in which the government of a country in the Middle East choreographed an event before CNN's television cameras so its pronouncements would reach the greater audience and have the maximum effect. During the Persian Gulf War, CNN had planned to carry live a 2:00 P.M. press conference by the country's secretary of state.

> From the control room here at CNN Center I could see the live satellite picture of the camera outside the door of this individual's office. The door was open and I could hear what was going on. As it turned out, President Bush was live on CNN at the same time and his comments were going beyond two o'clock. I turned up the speaker on the Middle East remote so I could listen in to know when the [official] was coming out, so I could brief the anchors. When I turned up the monitor, what did I hear but a television set in the office. They were listening to President Bush, whose statement went on until about 20 minutes after two. This leader sat and waited in his office knowing that he wouldn't get on the air so long as President Bush was speaking. Thirty seconds after the President finished, he came out, made his statement and took questions.[12]

√ Governments — especially the United States government — no longer can count on international media organizations such as CNN to cooperate with the press arrangements they have been accustomed to make during previous conflicts, according to Arnett. This was evident in CNN's response when President Bush and the Pentagon ordered all civilians, including the international press, out of Iraq prior to the bombing of Baghdad;

> The view of Ted Turner and CNN was, "Wait a minute. We are an international news organization. The world is interested in where those bombs are going to land and what is the effect." That's why we stayed in Baghdad.[13]

Although CNN President and CEO Tom Johnson has acknowledged that the network's coverage of abuses of power and the pictures it transmits around the world probably *do* shape

---

[12] Furnad, interview with Ghilardi (December 1996).

[13] Arnett, lecture (26 April 1996).

government policy, he said CNN does not set out to affect any specific policy.

> Images of the people dying in that Sarajevo marketplace when the mortar crashed in near the CNN cameras was a very important image which contributed to world attention. The images of the hundreds of thousands of dying refugees in Rwanda contributed, I think, to the U.S. attention and the United Nations attention. The images of the dying children in Somalia led to the humanitarian relief effort and unfortunate attacks on U.N. and U.S. forces. But again, our mission [at CNN] is not to influence world opinion. Our mission is to report and inform, not to be trying to influence public opinion. We do hope that as people are better informed through those images that they can make judgements about what should be done in the world arena.[14]

Yet, even for a news company that wants to operate in the "world arena," employing thousands of journalists and opening new bureaus as fast as the American broadcast networks are closing bureaus, being *comprehensive* in international news coverage is nearly impossible for practical as well as editorial reasons. News producers at CNN still tend to give "center-stage" coverage to certain world news events. While CNN is giving saturation coverage to one or two major international stories, many other events as a result are poorly covered or not covered at all. Rob Golden, who became an international assignment editor back in 1984 when there were only six staffers on the International Desk, described how this happens;

> It's generally true that most days of the year there is at least one lead story which we put special emphasis on. It could be Bosnia one day, Iraq the next, Rwanda the day after. Whichever story produces the sharpest developments, surprises, and drama will typically be the story we emphasize with interviews, correspondent reports, and live shots. However, the decision to focus on such stories is often limited by our access, technical abilities, and cost of covering a story. Today, for example, there's a lot of bloodshed in Somalia. It's a story we'd certainly like to explore. But we have no one in Somalia. No other journalist is reachable there. A

---

[14] Ibid.

dangerous place where only the bravest, or most stupid, journalists venture for any length of time. No working phones. No feed facilities. No working airport. In short, a nightmare to cover. So instead of Somalia, we are today placing greater emphasis on our Rwanda/Tanzania coverage.[15]

Stephen Cassidy, in meeting with a group of International Professional Program (IPP) trainees representing a dozen mostly developing countries, admitted being troubled by the fact that some stories get attention and others do not, that some places get noticed and others do not. He and his colleagues on the International Desk struggle with these issues every day, according to Cassidy.

> Remember the Zapatistas down in Mexico? Explain this to me. I couldn't understand this and had big fights with the people I work with on this. All the world is watching Bosnia, right, and there's great conflict there and great civil war going on, and then the Mexican government sends its air force to go and bomb its own poeple down in Chiapas, and the world didn't even pay any attention, It was like, uh? But if the French government had sent their air force down in the Côte d'Azu, it would have been gigantic headlines. If the United States had sent its air force to bomb Las Vegas, it would have been a gigantic story. But here's the Mexican government sending [its military] down to Chiapas, hundreds, thousands died, and nobody paid any attention to it. . . . We covered it, but it didn't get the big headlines. We'd bring the stories in and they'd play in the newscast, but they weren't like A-1 at five minutes. It was two minutes. And I wanted to send more reporters, I wanted to send a flyaway [satellite uplink], and people go, "Naw, it's not that important."[16]

Christiane Amanpour, one of CNN's best-known international correspondents and often among the first reporters at the scene to

---

[15] Rob Golden (assignment editor, CNN International Desk), interview (December 1996).

[16]Stephen Cassidy (senior international assignment editor, CNN), from comments made to CNN's International Professional Program participants (September 1996).

cover crises and wars for CNN,[17] confirmed that that's the way it is with international news.

> CNN, like any other international news organization, tries not to play favorites. In truth there are countries to which CNN returns time and time again and some countries to which we never go. African countries are examples. The most significant illustration of this was the Rwanda genocide in 1994. Everybody was late getting in there. For CNN, it was the year of O.J. and the attention of the company was focused elsewhere. Africa is a big continent.[18]

Amanpour said the reasons are mostly cultural. French reporters are in Africa more than CNN is, in part because it relates to their cultural history. But CNN has the same problems covering Arab/Islamic cultures. "It is the nature of news as we know it. The spotlight moves to some regions and not others; the spotlight stays longer in some places."[19]

When CNN focuses on a specific breaking story, it becomes the world's issue of the moment. According to Amanpour, whether in Serbia, Indonesia, China, or Saudi Arabia, the state may control the local media, but they cannot keep the citizens from receiving news and information from outside. During the December 1996 demonstrations in the streets of Belgrade, she noted, Serbian authorities had shut down coverage of the event by local media. But opposition leaders erected, in the downtown square, a huge television screen that carried the CNN signal. CNN's reporter coverage in the capital city and its satellite feeds to private dishes in the country were not blocked. Meanwhile, citizens protesting the voting irregularities of the Milosevic government were on the phone to Atlanta and firing off e-mail messages to CNN urging them to keep the spotlight on Yugoslavia.

---

[17] One newspaper reporter recently noted that "Amanpour is such a familiar presence in the world's trouble-spots that fellow journalists launch into a ditty whenever she touches down: 'Where there's a war, there's Amanpour.'" Lydia Slater, "The Ingenue Who Couldn't Wait To Go to War; Christiane Amanpour Is the World's Highest-paid Foreign Correspondent," *Daily Telegraph* (27 June 1996): 13.

[18] Christiane Amanpour, interview (November 1996).

[19] Ibid.

CNN's approach to covering news events—whether they occur in the U.S. or Serbia—more or less follows the same centralized model. The International Desk coordinates all of CNN's field reporters and producers, bringing into the system as many reports as possible. Those reports are then listed in CNN's computer system for the use of producers who select what reports to include in the networks' various newscasts. Depending on the audience for a network or show, producers will select stories geared toward their audience, or will write a script or tailor a piece of video or graphic information in ways that may be different from another CNN show or network.

One of CNN's 600 affiliates around the world may have a special interest in a story CNN is covering. When the hostage crisis broke in Lima, Peru, for example, the hundreds of people held hostage included diplomats from several countries, many Peruvians, Japanese businessmen, and several U.S. citizens. CNN domestic and Headline News, both seen in the United States, were particularly interested in the status of the U.S. citizens held within the compound and comments from the U.S. government on the situation.[20] CNN Spanish focused on the Latin American angle, highlighting the Latin American players involved. And TV Asahi, a key CNN affiliate, counted on CNN for help in covering this as a "Japan" story.

In such instances, a wide array of video and information elements are needed to satisfy all of the various "users" of the information, and the International Desk must coordinate the efforts of the crews on the ground to ensure the varying demands are satisfied. The CNN International Desk provides news material for the CNN networks in several forms:

- *video* (shot by CNN, its affiliates, or another source that supplies CNN with video, such as Video Reuters, WTN, APTV)

- *written information* (the International Desk calls sources worldwide and coordinates the efforts of CNN personnel overseas to gather facts on news stories worldwide and compiles them in an internal wire file for CNN writers and

---

[20] At the request of the U.S. State Department, CNN agreed not to air the fact that there were Americans in the compound for fear they might be singled out.

producers and affiliates to use when producing and writing news reports)

- *live or taped reports from correspondents and/or guests*

- *phone reports from correspondents and/or guests*

- *inhouse reports* (news reports written, voiced and edited in Atlanta or London for what CNN can't cover using a correspondent or stringer)

The International Desk must coordinate the activities of CNN's 20 non-U.S. bureaus, sending reporters and crews from one story to another and coordinating which stories they are going to cover and which live or phone (beeper) reports, if any, they are going to produce. When CNN reporters are unable, for whatever reason, to get to the scene of a news event, the International Desk attempts to contact government officials, non-government organizations, or even local businesses to get as much information as possible about the story, and if possible to arrange for them to appear on one of the CNN networks for a live phone interview.

## The Push to Internationalize

Golden recalled the period at CNN when the network finally was becoming profitable while still struggling to become a player in international news.

> Beginning in 1985, when CNN made its first attempts at international distribution, it was clear that the focus of the news was very much on American stories, with an American point of view. With very few exceptions, the only international stories we covered were ones in which there were U.S. strategic interests or U.S. familiarity. Yes, we covered events in Beirut and elsewhere in the mideast but hardly anything in the Indian subcontinent or Africa. We covered Nicaragua and the Falklands war but hardly anything else in South America and very little in Asia. We did not come close to satisfying a truly global coverage of events and issues.[21]

---

[21] Golden, interview (December 1996).

Within five years, CNN's international prospects had become far brighter. By the time Tom Johnson took over at CNN—just one day before Iraq's invasion of Kuwait—CNN was poised to become a global source for news about the war. Ted Turner had identified in Johnson a manager able to carry out the broadly stated directive to internationalize the company, a task that has become more like a *mission*:

> I think when CNN is there, there is greater public knowl-
> edge and attention. Frankly, I worry more about when CNN
> is not there, to shine a bright light into the very dark corners
> of the world [and] to look at issues even in democratic so-
> cieties such as the continued use of torture by the Israelis
> against those they interrogate, to disclose abuses of power
> in the United States in our own White House and among
> our leaders.[22]

In early 1996, Chris Cramer left the BBC as one of its top news executives to become a CNN International vice president, and a central figure in the company's conspicuous effort to interna-tionalize. As a relative newcomer to CNN, Cramer still marvels at CNN managers' faith in television news as a potential force for good;

> Being English, one is naturally skeptical about that kind of
> thinking, because it's very un-English. I actually believe that
> they are probably right. I think CNN *has* and *can* be a force
> for good, and I think that the type of television it produces
> has, over time, been exactly that.[23]

Those around Turner, and many who work for him, have a simi-lar vision, Cramer said. "It's not bullshit. It really isn't. I mean you can be cynical about it, but if you scratch it, it's not bullshit. It exists."[24] Still, according to Cramer, CNN's success owes more to its dogged pursuit of news in the western news tradition than to any "do-good" philosophy. Cramer described CNN as

> completely obsessive when it comes to being first. The word
> defeat does not exist in its vocabulary. I mean, failure

---

[22] Johnson, interview with Ghilardi (December 1996).

[23] Cramer (vice president, CNN International), interview (September 1996).

[24] Ibid.

doesn't exist in its vocabulary. There's a lot of Atlanta about that. There's a lot of boosterism about that, and the two are not unconnected.[25]

CNN appears to be equally determined to be ever more global in the coming years, perhaps an acknowledgment that the internationalization of the network is not yet complete. In the years since 1985, CNN has employed at least four distinct strategies to internationalize its newsgathering and news production operation:

- hiring a multi-national staff;

- building the company's international reputation for fairness, balance, accuracy, and sensitivity to local views;

- engaging in staff reorientation and training and developing a system of international protocol; and

- building linkages and cultivating international relationships, including taking full advantage of the resources and philosophy of *World Report*.

## International Hiring

CNN has made a "concerted effort to hire the very best journalists we can find all over the world," according to Eason Jordan, head of CNN International and a CNN vice president. One of the characteristics that Jordan said makes CNN distinctive is the increasing diversity of its workforce;

> You've got men and women, you've got black and white, you've got Arabs and Israelis, and you've got people from all over the world with Riz Khan being from Yemen and Sonia Ruseler being from Argentina and Ralitsa Vassileva being from Bulgaria, and Jonathan Mann being from Canada, literally from all over the planet making up our staff here in front of and behind the scenes.[26]

---

[25] Ibid.

[26] Eason Jordan (senior vice president, CNN), interview (August 1996).

The same holds true for the behind-the-scenes staff. Jordan noted that Cramer, the second-in-command at CNNI and "the guy who is really running CNN-International," is British. The 31 assignment editors who work on CNN's International Desk represent at least a dozen nationalities and speak some 20 languages.

David Clinch, an Atlanta-based assignment editor from Ireland, said the network's transformation into an international company necessitated an infusion of non-U.S. staffers.

> What is an international service? Who do we have at CNN who is going to do this for us? We didn't really have anybody. I wasn't here. The people who were running the International Desk were generally Americans with domestic network experience. Most were young with a concept of globalism but not necessarily the experience. So what happened again, as a kind of coincidence of what was needed, was the hiring of foreign people. So what do you end up with? You end up with an American service with a non-American influence which, by default, is an international service. I had never worked for a global news service. Neither had anybody else. What have you created? You have created an American service which was and still is American, with non-American influence which is as close to an international service as you can get.[27]

Clinch admitted to having many of the biases that come with being an Irish national. The key to being international was not to get rid of people with such biases, but to make sure that as many points of view are represented on the International Desk as possible.

> [International Assignment Editors] Yan Mei is Chinese and Kim Norgaard is Danish. Where is international? Is it somewhere out in the Atlantic Ocean? I don't know where it is. It is an extension of everybody in the world and you can never have everybody in the world working for CNN.[28]

This same principle applies to the field reporting task, because even though CNN's news producers do their work in Atlanta,

---

[27] David Clinch (assignment editor, CNN International Desk), inteview (December 1996).

[28] Ibid.

CNN news comes from a variety of sources—including local reporters from Europe, Asia, Latin America, and Africa. Paolo Ghilardi, an Italian graduate student completing an internship on the International Desk, remembered how CNN covered a breaking story in Italy by using local journalists;

> During the first days of my internship here in Atlanta, there was a crash of a Russian cargo plane in Turin, my home town. The way the International Desk covered it was to quickly locate someone in Turin to do a beeper for us. I helped locate the local journalist who covered the story. An American reporter would not likely have been there to cover the story or have been as familiar with the local situation. So even though it was CNN's story, it relied on local sources and had that flavor.[29]

## Training and Protocol

Lou Curles is director of protocol for TBS/CNN. Under that job description she is coordinator of major events, which includes *World Report* contributors conferences. Her job also entails coordinating visits of VIPs who come to CNN, setting up their meetings with various company executives, and arranging special tours of the newsroom.

> What I do first of all is find out if Tom Johnson is available. If he is not available, I go down the line. Ted is doing some [of the greeting] these days, but very rarely. Last year Ted did a lot of these. During the weeks and months prior to the Olympics we had many "pre-visits" from heads of state. This includes ambassadors and people of that stature. During the week before and the two weeks of the Olympics we had 924 VIPs come through CNN, most of whom Tom Johnson spoke to. We find an appropriate room in which to meet them. If they have secret service or state department people with them, [we] will meet them on the street level and bring them up. That is protocol. Tom will give an overview of CNN and many times call in the senior executives such as Eason Jordan and Bob Furnad. Then we take them on what

---

[29] Paolo Ghilardi (intern, CNN International Desk), interview (December 1996).

> we call the "executive tour," led by Tom Johnson and my
> staff. Each visit we try to design according to the interests
> they have, whether it's a look at CNN Interactive, CNN
> Sports Illustrated, CNN International, or in many cases just
> an overview of CNN.[30]

On the day she was interviewed for this book Curles was responding to a request from the king of Sweden, scheduled to visit Atlanta in March 1997. During the 1996 Summer Olympic Games, Curles coordinated visits to CNN for royalty such as Queen Sophia of Spain and the crown prince of Nepal, as well as high-level government officials from around the world.

The goal of Curles's work is relationship building. Her role is to help create new relationships for the company and to cement established relationships. In many cases, this requires sensitizing CNN's own staff to international issues and giving them the social tools with which to carry on successful international relationships.

> This past year my office put together a book to help with
> this. The CNN International Protocol manual has now been
> distributed to our executives and anyone else throughout
> the company who wants to use it. It has information on
> every country with which we have relationships. To use one
> example, the country of Greece, our affiliates and clients are
> listed in there, the geographic and cultural information, the
> "dos and don'ts" of that country, the things we want to talk
> about with them. This manual was done strictly for our
> needs in our company and is continually updated.[31]

According to Curles, the transformation of the network into an internationally-minded company — one capable of performing its international newsgathering responsibilities in an efficient and effective manner — required a more considered and professional approach to protocol.

> It has been very hard. As you know, many of the staff were
> here when the company was thought of as the Chicken
> Noodle Network, a kind of mom and pop operation.

---

[30] Lou Curles (director of international protocol, TBS/CNN), interview (December 1996).

[31] Ibid.

Ambassadors would come and just anybody would take them around, whoever knew them or was available. In 1994, Tom Johnson and Julia Sprunt looked into the need. I went on board in this capacity in 1995 and for the first months did try to sit down and see what we needed to do to educate our company, and of course with the merger we have had hopes of having many seminars and meetings to tell our executives what to do. Many of them of course know what to do; many do not.[32]

# Relationship-Building

A key component of the network's corporate and journalistic relationship-building strategy is CNN's *World Report*. When it comes to using local reporters to help gather the news and tell it on CNN, *World Report* is in the forefront. This willingness to turn over CNN air to reporters from contributing stations on a regular basis represents a kind of handshake, an agreement to listen to one another and share information, video, and other resources, so that a much more global and diverse newscast is the result.

The importance of the assignment editor for contributors cannot be underestimated, according to Stewart Krohn, general manager for TV Belize and a contributor to *World Report*. Krohn said it was because CNN "asked me nicely" that he decided to become a contributor. The person responsible for bringing Krohn into the CNN family was Debra Daugherty, an assignment editor since 1992;

> Some projects take weeks, months, years to bear fruit. During a trip to South America, I met with the owners of Uruguay's Saeta TV and Mexico's Multivision News. On returning to Atlanta, I followed up with both stations making phone calls, writing letters and sending contributor kits. In each case, the 'yes' came nine months later.[33]

*World Report* assignment editors often are the first CNN personnel to make contact with emerging broadcast stations or organizations around the world, according to Andrew Henstock, an

---

[32] Ibid.

[33] Debra Daugherty (assignment editor, *World Report*), interview (February 1997).

assignment editor who first joined *World Report* as an intern after taking a journalism course in graduate school.[34]

> Within the past couple of years we have started working with newly formed private companies in both Africa and in the former Soviet Union. We used to work with TASS, so when the Soviet Union split up, we had to fill in all the blanks there. We had to go out and find [potential contributors] from Belarus, the Ukraine, and the Baltics, all the former republics. The trouble is finding English speakers in place. They are at a premium, especially in the former Soviet republics. When you make that first phone call, it is always fun cold calling.[35]

One of the most effective approaches employed by *World Report* assignment editors when soliciting contributors for news reports is to emphasize that such reports can change viewers' perspectives on an entire region or people. Assignment Editor Octavia Nasr said she believes that her success is largely a measure of her ability to get contributors to see *World Report* as a valuable vehicle for communicating their views:

> It took me a long time to get people [from the Middle East] to start contributing, because of the mistrust. There was ignorance of the culture. The Middle East seems to a lot of people such a far-away land. A lot of people think of it as nomadic or a desert, or people with camels, they ride camels to work and park their camels outside, something like this. And the Arabs *feel* that.
>
> When I started [here] no one wanted stories from the Middle East because they were all, [by] some standards, "boring." But what these people did not think of then was that the Middle East was not taking *them* seriously. So they were sending their third-class reporting. They were sending it to *World Report* because they didn't pay much attention to

---

[34] Andrew Henstock (assignment editor, *World Report*), interview (August 1996). Henstock, from Scotland, recalled that "one of my first exposures to *World Report*, the first time I had actually seen it, was in a graduate seminar. We were addressing the whole idea of news flow, NWIO, and all that. It caught my interest and I came here as an intern."

[35] Ibid.

*World Report.* They didn't think that *World Report* was such a great idea then.

> But then they realized that if they send a good piece, this piece is going to take a good spot in the show, it's going to be introduced right, it's going to air so many times, the point of view is going to be there. If it's a bad piece, people are going to think, "Oh, Kuwait TV, they don't produce good pieces." If it's a strong piece, people are going to say, "Wow, look at what Kuwait TV can do." Then, instead of just waiting for them to do stories, you start calling them, saying, "I *want* you to do a story for me. I really want the Kuwaiti perspective in this."[36]

CNN's *World Report* efforts in Africa—always an underrepresented, underreported region of the world—are likely to produce still more broadcasting partners for CNN. According to Henstock, this is primarily because of Africa's changing media environment.

> In a lot of [African] countries, like Nigeria, their systems just got deregulated. We work with the mouthpiece of the state NTA but we've also got three more private Nigerian stations. . . . They take a very different view of events than the state station. In fact, it spurs the state station to do a few more reports just because they've got those other [private contributors] there . . . that are less afraid of addressing issues than the state station.[37]

In the early years of *World Report*, its founding editor, Stuart Loory, was chief ambassador for the program. More recently the assignment editors have assumed that role, to the benefit of the entire CNN network, according to Nasr:

> It's very interesting and I am very happy [to serve as CNN's representative]. I am proud of that because CNN calls on me for lots of things, from attending conferences and signing contracts or renewing contracts. When we run into

---

[36] Octavia Nasr (assignment editor, *World Report*), interview (September 1996). Nasr, a former contributor to *World Report* from Lebanon, also said that her experience as a contributor, "having been in their shoes, helps a lot. I don't ask them for things that are impossible." For Nasr, this means understanding what is "reasonable" to ask, "the thing that I would have done if I were in their shoes."

[37] Henstock, interview (August 1996).

trouble with a certain contract in the Arab world, I go. There was one time where Eason didn't even think that we were going to get anywhere but he said "Just go anyway and try." Believe it or not, I pulled out my Arabic proverbs and ways, like, "If you do me this favor, we are going to save our relationships." It worked. It was beautiful. . . . It makes you feel that next time I need these people, it's going to be much easier to request things. It just builds great relationships, not only for *World Report*, but for CNN as well.[38]

Daugherty said that the assignment editors' *World Report* contacts in particular regions of the world make them valuable to the network's push to internationalize:

For several years, I have attended the General Assembly of the Caribbean Broadcasting Union. The two-day meeting allows me to recruit new stations and to spend time with Caribbean news managers reinforcing year-round contact by phone. The presence of CNN and CNN World Report is seen by the CBU board as a strong sign of support for their union. One-on-one contact with CNN World Report contributors has always netted year-round results with new contacts and contributors.[39]

## *World Report* Newsgathering

Shortly after *World Report*'s launch in 1987, Scott Shuster noted in the *Columbia Journalism Review* the potential for contributors to the *World Report* program to displace conventional "foreign correspondents" who cover "foreign news" for the American news media.[40] Now that an estimated 20,000 news reports have been added into CNN's mix of news, it must be acknowledged that *World Report* does function as an important adjunct to international newsgathering, and the expectations of World Report news grows increasingly closer to expectations of CNN-reported news.

---

[38] Nasr, interview (September 1996).

[39] Debra Daugherty (assignment editor, *World Report*), interview (September 1996).

[40] Scott Shuster, "Foreign Competition Hits the News," *Columbia Journalism Review* 27 (May 1988): 43-45.

What makes *World Report*'s newsgathering apparatus ~ ing is the unique manner in which its assignment editors inter~ with potential reporters in the field. The producers who transform individually contributed reports into weekend and daily *World Report* shows rely on a staff of assignment editors to coax contributors into providing timely stories with good video, understandable narration, and most importantly, local perspectives on issues or events which will capture the interest and attention of CNN's viewers worldwide. The *World Report* staff expanded from three to four assignment editors in early 1996, which has produced more diversity in the news programming because "we can take the time to recruit and solicit packages from places that have not been heard from," according to Daugherty.[41]

Each of the four assignment editors communicates with contributing journalists in designated regions of the world. But unlike their counterparts on CNN's international assignment desk, *World Report* assignment editors have no direct authority over a staff of reporters. Instead, they must rely on personal relationships and on understanding and commitment to the unique philosophy of the program in working with the journalists who contribute reports for the daily and weekend *World Report* shows. Given the constraints, assignment editors often resort to playing the role of cheerleader, sometimes with unexpected results, according to Claudia Chang, a recent addition to the assignment editing staff at *World Report*:

> I was just talking to a new reporter from one of our [contributing stations] in Taiwan. He is interested in doing some stories about the growing social problems in Taiwan . . . . While he believes in Taiwan and he is proud of it, he does also want to point out that with all the growth of democracy, with all these flourishing economics, there are still some problems that they are experiencing—a larger underworld crime organization system, a lot more drug-trafficking is going on. . . . He would call them growing pains. He is very excited about doing that. If that's the aspect he wants to look at, I support what he wants to do. I haven't at all been concerned that contributors may not know what

---

41 Daugherty, interview (September 1996).

they are going to put themselves into. They definitely know.[42]

Each week, the four assignment editors phone journalists in their respective regions to determine whether reports will be filed, and more commonly in recent years, to offer story ideas and suggestions for coverage. Conversations between assignment editors and contributors are negotiations, rarely if ever turning into the type of confrontation that can occur between assignment editors and reporters. Nasr said the process is not unlike "selling old cars."

> The good ones are the ones that want to work with you and say, "What can I do to get the best spot on the show?" "What can I do to lead the show?" If I feel that [a topic] is going to be the lead story, I call up [the reporter] and I say, "This is a lead." I guarantee that she will do it. When you tell her that it's going to lead the show, she will put extra effort into it, a lot more effort into it. It's funny the way it works. It's like you are representing these people and you know exactly how they are thinking and you know exactly their limitations and you know that . . . if you tell them, "I really need this piece, I want this perspective on the show because I am getting the other two perspectives, you are the only one missing and this block is going to be the lead of the show," you know she is going to do it.[43]

And when the process is complete, feedback from the *World Report* staff helps improve both the relationship with contributors and the quality of their work, according to Nasr.

> You see good results from the feedback, from giving them ideas and telling them how things can be done. But not dictating, definitely not dictating. Or making them change their customs or their ways of doing things. . . . You're not telling them what to do, but you're telling them, "if you use a little less of all this, you know, graphic movement there, maybe the story is told in a better way. It's being understood in a better way, because people need to focus.[44]

---

[42] Claudia Chang (assignment editor, *World Report*), interview (September 1996).

[43] Ibid.

[44] Ibid.

Even as the number of *World Report* assignment editors grows and they become more aggressive as newsgatherers, there are constant reminders of where the lines are drawn, according to Henstock:

> We get paid to do this. They don't. We try not to lose sight of that when we are dealing with [contributors]. I try not to forget that I am asking someone to do something on a day off or during their spare time. I think that's important. The minute I start demanding stuff, that is probably the minute they'll decide it's not a good idea to do it.[45]

Nasr added that working at *World Report* requires having a special understanding of what contributors have to offer, and how much trouble they go to to contribute;

> Jordan TV doesn't have a whole crew [devoted to *World Report*]. IBA doesn't have a whole crew for me. No. These people, after they do their jobs, they are doing me favors. They are putting pieces together, giving us their beepers. You know, all these things. So, if you don't understand this, you are in the wrong business.[46]

Nasr also said that, while the assignment editors and producers sometimes want contributors to send in a particular story, produced from a particular angle, or incorporating particular techniques, boundaries still exist and must be observed, even while helping contributors improve their work. Chang agreed.

> You really have to be very open in how you think about what should be coming. That word "should" is just the most difficult one because you think about what we like, what can happen, the time under which it can happen, the resources under which it can happen. That affects what you are going to be getting and that's not specifically defined.[47]

It is this kind of sensitivity that differentiates the role of the *World Report* assignment editor from a conventional television news assignment editor, said Henstock, as well as the omnipresent fact that the lack of a financial relationship between

---

[45] Henstock, interview (August 1996).

[46] Nasr, interview (September 1996).

[47] Chang, interview (September 1996).

CNN and contributors means the two act more like partners in gathering the news;

> For most other organizations, as in CNN, you work on a money basis. You do a phone interview and you get paid so many dollars. As an assignment editor, you assign something and you expect it to be completed the way you assign it. Here it is not really like that. It is a request, not a demand. That is the difference. If I say [to the Russian contributor], "We would like something on General [Alexander] Lebed," for example, and the Russian contributor said: "That is not really the story. I think this is the story," then we go with that.[48]

## *World Report* and CNN Converge

*World Report* assignment editors are expected to keep a constant flow of reports coming in to Atlanta—an expectation that has changed little since the days when Loory was executive producer. Yet the *way* in which these newsgatherers function has changed dramatically. When Donna Mastrangelo became executive producer of the program in 1991, she reorganized the *World Report* staff, borrowing the "assignment editor" model from her local television news background. The *World Report* assignment editor assumed a more activist role in soliciting material. According to Nasr,

> Before Donna, newsgathering was not newsgathering really. It was just calling contributors up and saying "What do you have for me this week?" [We'd receive] a mishmash of reports that we'd have to put together for the show. Because [Donna] worked on a newsgathering desk, she had a very good understanding of newsgathering. And, she turned it around [so] that we go after stories. "You read the paper. This is the big story. This is what you want on the show. Get the contributors on."[49]

The assignment editors' activist role also had an impact on *World Report*'s production standards, creating an atmosphere in which

---

[48] Henstock, interview (September 1996).

[49] Nasr, interview (September 1996).

*World Report* producers Scott Herron and Susan Winé could embrace the premise of the program applying conventional television production standards.

The role of the show producer in television news is not generally understood by viewers, who naturally focus on reporters and anchors. Yet show producers shape the content of news programs, acting as gatekeepers of the news, determining the order of the stories as they attempt to assemble a "watchable" newscast. News stories are clustered together into segments, along with "teases" and "bumps" intended to keep viewers tuned in despite the constant interruption of advertisement breaks.

Unlike traditional TV news producers, *World Report* producers theoretically have no control over contributors' scripts, nor can they pick up a phone and threaten to have a contributor fired because of a poorly constructed package. But in the same way that *World Report*'s assignment editors use personal persuasion to get contributors to send in packages, the program's two show producers—one for the two-hour Sunday program and another for the daily show—use their own influence to get reporters to conform to particular production guidelines and stylistic conventions of television news. Such conventions include using natural sound to complement video, reporter "stand-ups"[50] (but no more than one per package), and scripts that make sense and are delivered in understandable English.

*World Report*'s current approach to news was plainly evident on Sunday, November 4 1995—the first "live" weekend show ever—when the program led not with a contributor to *World Report* but with a story from Walter Rogers, CNN bureau chief in Jerusalem. The report concluded with a Q&A exchange between *World Report* Anchor/Executive Producer Ralph Wenge and Rogers. What was remarkable about the report was how similar it was to conventional CNN fare. Viewers would notice little difference between that report and what they usually viewed on CNN, perhaps causing *World Report*'s contributing journalists to wonder why the program, which for most of its ten years televised

---

[50] Sometimes called a "stand-upper," this is the part of the videotaped report in which the reporter is seen speaking directly to the viewer.

"unedited, uncensored reports from the perspective of the world's broadcasters," had begun to look less and less like unconventional *World Report* and more CNN-like.[51]

In the early years of *World Report*, any attempt to exert pressure — subtle or not — on *what* a contributor submitted was seen as risky — and perhaps a violation of the original agreement CNN made to contributors, which precluded the network from dictating what could be sent. From time to time, when a particularly one-sided report was contributed, Loory and his staff would inform another contributor that such a report had been received. The *World Report* staff would express willingness to receive a report expressing contrary views. In the case of South Africa, Loory even made exceptions to his own rule about who could be a contributor, allowing a production company — New York–based *South Africa Now* — to contribute reports that balanced the views presented by the SABC, South Africa's main broadcast company. Assuring that multiple perspectives were aired was an important consideration.

While certain rules are absolute — no packages will air if they are longer than two and a half minutes, and longer packages will be edited down — other efforts by the show producers to shape the program are more subtle. Susan Winé, the Sunday show producer, encourages contributors to submit scripts for advance review, while Herron, the daily show producer, evaluates packages from established broadcasters by a different standard than the one he applies to contributions from less-experienced and less-equipped stations, the latter getting the benefit of the doubt because of their circumstances. Technically speaking, all reports are to be aired, provided they meet the agreed-upon minimum standards. However, packages that appeal to the producers will get better — and more frequent — play, being featured in a segment near the beginning of the show, or being aired on both the

---

[51] Wenge explained that, when it was determined that *World Report*'s contributors in Israel were unavailable, busy working on the breaking story for their own news organizations, CNN President Tom Johnson suggested that Rogers be used — an exception to the program's policy of not using CNN reporters in such instances. Ralph Wenge (executive producer, *World Report*), interview (December 1996).

Sunday and the daily show. And packages that are technically unusable sometimes can be salvaged by a CNN editor—always with the contributor's permission.

Over the years, it should be noted, the relationship between the Atlanta-based *World Report* staff and the contributors around the world has become more cooperative. The program has become as much an Atlanta-based production as it once was a contributor-based production. As assignment editors become more aggressive in seeking out reports, and as show producers become more active in shaping reports to fit the program goals, *World Report* must be seen as more of a partnership. This has meant that the program's weekend and daily show producers work hard at improving each show's pacing and variety, specifically to avoid the "intro-package-intro-package-intro-package" pattern that is thought to make *World Report* less appealing to viewers accustomed to American TV news.

One way Winé and Herron attempt to avoid such a predictable pattern is to intersperse brief voice-over (VO) reports, in which the anchor reads the script while the viewer sees video, between the two-minute-thirty-second packages. VO reports are generated by editing down packages that exceed the time limit and by pulling text and video from international news feeds and wire services (e.g., AP, UPI, and Reuters) to strengthen the stories and enhance viewer interest. This practice has become common. Current show producers operate more like their counterparts on the CNN domestic and CNN International news programs than like their predecessors at *World Report*, who mainly "stacked" the program with whatever packages were available.

Herron, a former CNNI writer and self-described internationalist, argued that his task as the daily show producer is to create a half-hour program that "makes sense" sandwiched as it is between two other CNN news programs. To Herron, this means creating a program that adds the contributors' perspectives to breaking stories from their country or region. In the past, a supervising producer at CNNI likely would have preempted the daily *World Report* show to cover the breaking story using CNN's own staff of reporters and analysts. To avoid being "blown out of the water," according to Herron and executive producer Ralph

Wenge, the daily—and even the weekend *World Report* pro-gram—has adopted what might be referred to as a "beeper" mode, whereby contributors are interviewed by telephone much in the same way that CNN reporters often give their eyewitness account of an event by phone.

Herron and Winé acknowledged that their attempts to be as current as possible can sometimes backfire, given that their pro-grams are re-aired from tape several hours after the initial live telecast. When the United States naval forces fired cruise missiles at radar stations in southern Iraq, Herron's show for the day in-cluded six live interviews (by phone) with contributors in the Middle East. He opened the show with a set-up piece that incor-porated a script he had written, covered by video of cruise mis-siles being launched from the U.S. ships. The combination of script and video looked entirely conventional, as did the replay-ing of the video during the beepers from the six contributors. In effect, there was nothing about the set-up piece remotely intrinsic to *World Report*, and it was clear that Herron's traditional news instincts honed during years at CNNI had overtaken him. Herron and Wenge saw this strategy as a way to keep the program from being preempted by a CNNI supervising producer. They were thus able to accomplish their goal of getting the perspective of *World Report* contributors from the Middle East onto CNN air.[52]

CNNI's Chris Cramer has noted the changes in *World Report*, and generally likes what he sees.

> I am actually very impressed with how it's developed over the years. Because it *has* developed over the years. *World Report* is not a passive product. It doesn't simply pick up re-ports and write leads and put them on the air. We weave them into a particular vehicle, which has the potential to remain always up to date.[53]

---

[52] Herron and Wenge said assignment editors, when arranging the live tele-phone interviews, urge the contributors to focus on analysis and background issues, and not on the breaking event itself. Interviews (August, September 1996).

[53] Cramer, interview (September 1996).

That doesn't stop him from worrying that *World Report* occasionally is becoming *too* CNN-like. And CNN's president and CEO, Tom Johnson, remains cautious about the use of *World Report* contributors for conventional newsgathering for the network, in part because of the appearance that CNN unfairly benefits from the work of its broadcasting partners;

> I often repeat that we do not intend to use the *World Report* conference or the IPP program as a recruitment system, and I really mean that. These efforts should be done to help the local broadcasters to build their own stations and improve their own services to the nations they serve.[54]

But clearly, *World Report* does enhance CNN's reputation as an internationally-minded newsgathering operation, even if only by giving the traditionalists at the network a better argument to use when defending the network against charges of being too American. At the conference on media coverage of war, Arnett used *World Report* to illustrate how the network offered broadcasters from Arab countries an equal opportunity to present their side of the Arab-Israeli conflict.[55] Cassidy, of CNN's International Desk, went even further in underscoring *World Report*'s potential newsgathering value in that it would allow CNN to cover the world more completely, more comprehensively;

> We are limited. We have limited resources just like anybody else. Limited number of people, limited amount of money. That's why a greater number of news organizations help you get a better picture of what's going on in the world. I spend CNN money over here, [contributors] spend money over there. Maybe by working together everybody sort of gets it covered.[56]

Managers like Cassidy said they acknowledge the obvious benefits to the news company of having a network of contributors around the world, ready and willing to help CNN cover world events in their respective backyards. But these same managers also worry that *World Report*'s uniqueness will be jeopardized by

---

[54] Johnson, interview (December 1996).

[55] Arnett, lecture (26 April 1996).

[56] Cassidy, from comments made to CNN's International Professional Program participants (September 1996).

being associated too closely with the International Desk. On the other hand, such closeness arguably will make CNN's on-air product all the more compelling as it prepares for the first real competition in the international arena.

THE GLOBAL VILLAGE WENT ON-LINE *yesterday, as its far-flung clan chieftans, from Bill Clinton to Yitzhak Rabin to Yasser Arafat, hooked into satellite press conferences run from the new CNN international centre in Atlanta, and beamed out simultaneously to 141 countries.*[*]

Martin Walker
*The Guardian*

---

[*] "Nation Speaks Unto Nation—Via CNN," *The Guardian* (4 May 1994):9.

# 5

# The Push of Technology

*We have perfected the art of stumbling forward.*[1]

Scott Teissler is a vice president in charge of new media strategy and infrastructure for CNN. Ken Tiven is a vice president in charge of television systems. They were hired to examine how things are done at CNN, ask why they are done that way, and to propose alternative technological approaches for keeping the company competitive.

The following exchange was recorded during a December 1996 meeting in which the two vice presidents were brainstorming about technological challenges confronting the news business, and in particular about the challenges and opportunities for CNN. At the time, Tiven and Teissler had become convinced that CNN could pursue a wider range of stories more effectively and at less expense if the company re-examined some widely-held assumptions about technology.

*Teissler:*

> We almost gather news by appointment. You've got all that equipment and a crew to take. You want to know in advance what you are going to get when you go there and you don't want to spend a lot of time looking for it.

*Tiven:*

> We all agree we ought to drill more dry holes. You go out and pursue a story and it doesn't work, but 10 people

---

[1] Ken Tiven (vice president for television systems, CNN), interview (December 1996).

pursuing 10 stories may be a better content decision than 10 people pursuing two stories because it takes five people to work each story. Another way to look at it is that we tend to have a one-size-fits-all approach to news coverage — betacam, cameraman, sound person, reporter, producer — that goes after big stories and little stories.

If indeed it all comes down to content, if you can never have too much content, CNN should have a larger number of bureaus with more people in the field. What we would like to do is dramatically increase our capacity for coverage. Then, what we would have is more things to choose from and less repetition of interior content. . . . If the TWA 800 goes down off Long Island, that's not going to become a tertiary story on the third day. But there are all kinds of interior stories that could be shifted and changed and re-focused. . . .

That's a function of creating, out of enormous technological advances, capabilities that we don't have now. There's a new JVC video camera-recorder that's the size of this [he points to the audio recorder] that costs $3000 and alleged to make the picture twice as good as VHS. We want to know whether in a setting [like the TWA crash] this equipment is good enough to gather a whole lot more information, even though in the finished piece you only use a nine-second soundbite. If you can get all that information, plus your soundbite, without dragging a two-person betacam crew to this event, then your piece would have greater content than it would otherwise have, and perhaps greater economy.

CNN is the global standard for 24-hour news. Our brand name suggests a high level of competency and fairness. We do that well and people understand that. And everywhere there is a crisis our audience rises like a rocket. The problem is it falls back to the gravitational pull of mediocrity when we get out of the breaking-news business. So somehow we need to strengthen our capabilities and make the "wonderment" factor of small stories go up.

*Teissler:*

We have some evidence from the on-line world that this theory is on the mark. The Internet statistics are admittedly more developed here in the U.S., but we have got studies that suggest that a lot of people consume interactive content in the workplace. When wired into the Internet, even when the big news isn't actually changing that rapidly, these people visit the Turner and Time Warner sites several times a day. They are getting some kind of gratification from sampling those sites, so if there are more elements of novelty and surprise, something more than just a better rendering of AP [newswire], that tendency would probably continue.

It is not obvious to me why you need to check the CNN-Interactive three or four times a day. We think, in the context of the present Interactive, it is because the content is changing relatively rapidly, because we are doing a large number of stories on air, because shelf space is infinite. That suggests there are improvements in this so-called internal content that resonate with some of our news consumers.

*Tiven:*

It becomes increasingly clear in the last few years of this millennium that the things that are really important to own are the newsgathering skills and the distribution pipeline. What's in between those is the sort of show biz form and style of it all and we can probably figure out how to manage that for whatever niche we want. We really need to have assets on the ground gathering information, getting stuff firsthand. Luckily, we have built a sort of slice-and-dice facility here [in Atlanta] that takes the core material and spits it out for lots of people.

I really believe that in 1998 we will stand on virtually any acre on the face of the earth and with a device not much bigger than a hand-held tape player—a type of cellular telephone with enough bandwidth to store and forward video in a realistic amount of time—to cover the news in broadcast quality.

*Teissler:*

It's also a space in which we don't get a lot of choice in participating. A good analogy might be something that is happening now—within the context of the [World Wide] Web—we have a site but other people have sites which incorporate elements of our site all or in part. Now the legality of all this is in question. Our position is clear, that they ought not to do that, but the fact is our kind of content can be harvested and re-rendered on the Web and Web-like things.

Whether the transport medium is a satellite system or something else doesn't really matter, if there is a demand for our content and the transport system will get it there, it is going to be there, whether we put it there intentionally or somebody else does that for us, it will be done. Currently, our strategy has been pretty successful. As new transport schemes, distribution schemes, interactive schemes, whatever their constraints are, if one of those looks like it is going to go, we try to be there early, and establish whatever the standard is for news there. It makes it tougher for whoever follows.

### Tiven:

We have a tendency to see a pyramid, and at the top of the pyramid is a CNN news crew someplace in the world producing a package for CNN which is then dismembered and re-used all the way down through the food chain. It is entirely reasonable that a year from now we will have people with electronic still cameras at $150 to $500 a pop for the camera producing a series of still images and narration track delivering it on the Internet to the Website where it is repackaged into a finished piece and if it is interesting enough and good enough it might find its way onto television.

I don't believe it is a top-down process. I think the real growth for news on the Internet is when the Internet starts sending out its own reporters with its own tool set, using the computing skills and the networking capabilities of the internet to do whatever it does in the same way that in our generation in our lifetime we watched radio news guys turn into television news guys and the evolution of the television news formats. Why would we think re-purposing television onto Web pages is some fine art? It is embryonic crawling out of this primordial soup towards land stage of the Web. The Web is going to get a lot slicker, and a lot more satisfying.

### Teissler:

[Viewers] come to us. If you took the brand potency and divided it by the size of the underlying enterprise, you divide CNN this year by $750 million and Coke you divide by $6 billion, whatever, that ratio would probably be higher for CNN than in any other . . . in terms of brand for underlying dollar of revenue.

*Tiven:*

People beat a path to our door if they have got a delivery innovation, because an innovation with us can give that innovation critical mass in the market with critical support. [CNN] is presently viewed as an important enabler in this [Internet] space. It can legitimize new content forms, it can establish an initial audience, a promotional venue. . . .

The difference is—and it's really a fascinating one—CNN is a 24-hour multichannel enterprise. Virtually all of our competitors do news as a tack-on to entertainment networks. So in the context of these other guys, they don't have much canvas space, they don't have a lot of room to manipulate. NBC [and] CBS in 1996 have come to understand that CNN has become the brand name that you hear and see and it resonates as news, as Coke does with the soft drink.

## Technology Solutions

CNN is not in the hardware business, but it is absolutely dependent on hardware to get it where it wants to go. The information business is competitive. Technology offers a needed edge, whether in reach, response time, capacity, or efficiency—all daily goals of news managers.

For CNN, technology means reaching customers and clients wherever they are, including international affiliates, cable operators, or home viewers. It means being first at the scene to cover the story and first to get that information back to Atlanta where editorial decisions are made and production and packaging are completed. And, of course, it means being first to air. It means delivering information in sufficient quantity and choice, in the right format, and in the right time frame, to meet customer need. And finally it means conducting business with greater efficiency in terms of effort and cost.

In the international news business, the technologies employed can sometimes be very basic. When a home-quality VHS camera is the only one recording a breaking news story, as happened with coverage of the fall of the Berlin Wall, armed conflict in the mountains of Afghanistan, boat people in Haiti, and the Olympic Park bombing in Atlanta, those are the images that will be used. When no satellite trucks are in the field to bring back signals from Angola, Chechnya, or East Timor, videotaped reports are hand-carried to the post office and mailed, or expressed by air courier when available, which may take days, but the images still have value.

The news business also employs technologies that can be very complex. The equipment may or may not work, or will work under certain conditions but not others, a condition requiring specially trained staff. The risk is very high that state of the art equipment will not be compatible with existing — and possibly future — equipment, and that there will be a format change which threatens to make the technology obsolete immediately following its purchase.

At CNN, which promises its audiences timely global news coverage, sophisticated technologies are required in support of some 3,000 news professionals, 30 bureaus, and 600 broadcast affiliates. CNN's telecommunications capabilities include both Intranet — an in-house, proprietary computer network — and Internet access, and access to the global telephone and satellite grid, which works better in some parts of the world than in others. CNN's newsroom technology — which includes a computer system for taking in newswire feeds and writing news stories for air, as well as video editing equipment to create pictures to accompany the words — is halfway between the trusted, reliable analog systems and the state-of-the-art digital systems, which will allow CNN personnel in control rooms, editing suites, video libraries, and newsrooms to share huge volumes of video, audio, graphic, and text data in a common format.

But utilizing new technologies has always heralded unexpected journalistic concerns and pragmatic challenges. Going live from the scene — a routine journalistic task in CNN's world — is "a high wire act that takes some steady hands to avoid mistakes," according to President and CEO Tom Johnson.[2] Lee Hall of *Electronic Media* recently predicted that

> The broadcast networks and their affiliates will face new pressure to pre-empt entertainment programming when a big story breaks. Local stations are increasingly involved in covering stories of national scope, from the TWA crash to the Olympics bombing in Atlanta, joining in the daunting task of making split-second decisions about what's information and misinformation. And instant analysis is unlikely to produce good answers. The cause of the TWA crash and the culprit and motive for the Olympics bombing are still unknown despite on-air guesses and theories.[3]

If this is a problem for local and national news, it is a major challenge in the international arena where news crews are in less familiar territory.

## Satellites and Circuits

Dick Tauber, vice president for satellites and circuits, is one of the people at CNN whose job it is to match emerging technology to business opportunity. Tauber and his staff face nightmare conditions 24 hours a day as stories such as the hostage crisis in Peru unfold and the proper equipment is not available, or fails to work as promised. It is difficult enough to feed quality video out of a CNN bureau in Bangkok or Moscow or Mexico City where there are satellite uplinks and high capacity terrestrial lines, but to get good pictures back from wherever a story may develop is a tall order. To accomplish this with speed, economy, and good pictures is a minor miracle.

According to Tauber, CNN "wanted to add [digital] compression equipment a year ago but there was nothing out there that we could count on." He related the history of failures of the different technical formats in the satellite distribution business that promise to squeeze from two to eight signals onto a single

---

[2] Quoted in Lee Hall, "Breaking Live: A Moment of Truth for TV News," *Electronic Media* (7 October 1996): 32.

[3] Ibid.

transponder, or channel. The first commercial satellite network to provide near-global coverage, PanAmSat, bought and threw out several digital compression schemes and the equipment along with them, Tauber said. PanAmSat's business plan required that six to eight channels of programming had to be carried by each satellite transponder in order to make any profit. "The reason CNN stayed away from digital stuff up until now is that the quality level of the picture once compressed is not acceptable." He said the company made deals with a variety of vendors but did not like the result. CNN wanted to have the best quality,

> but more than just for us. It was important for our customers, who are going to have to edit and process that video. You can discard information from the digital picture [to make video more economical to transport] but the [affiliates and other users] have to have good pictures to work with.[4]

"Here is my soundbite for the day: compression is subtraction," according to Tauber. The advantage of an all-digital system is that all of the analog-to-digital and digital-to-analog conversions can be eliminated. In the case of compressed video, every one of those conversion steps causes a loss of data. Tauber said CNN may have jumped too soon when it tried in 1996 to move its Headline News unit toward digital non-linear editing, with a view toward creating the so-called *tapeless* newsroom. Under this system, video is stored and processed on massive computer hard drives the way words are stored and processed on a PC or Mac. But a lot of time and money was lost when the production system failed to live up to what was promised.[5]

Tauber said he *is* looking forward to the day when studio and transmission standards are integrated, he said. Currently, "the transmission side of it is still as confused as the non-linear side. They need to be coming off the same tree." Eventually, digital should flow into digital, computer to TV, TV to computer,

---

[4] Dick Tauber (vice president for satellites and circuits, CNN), interview (August 1996).

[5] One of the problems, aside from the obvious ones related to digital technology, is that in the CNN world of 24-hour news, there never is a chance to pause for training. As one Headline News staffer put it at the time, "It's like trying to change to another bicycle while you're still riding one at breakneck speed!"

according to Tauber; "everything flows in and out of itself. You stay digital from camera to set-top box, if it all works right."[6] Two new CNN networks, CNN*fn* and CNN-SI, began as digital networks in 1996, and CNN en Español expanded to a 24-hour service in 1997. And Tauber said he has money in his budget to begin transmission in digital, adding equipment in the London, Moscow, Jerusalem, and Hong Kong bureaus. Now satellite signals feed into and out of London one channel at a time;

> Once the compression equipment is in, we will maximize our satellite resources [feeding multiple streams in multiple directions] in a way we have not done up to this point. It may take two or three years before we can wean away from the analog side of the business and just go up digital. . . . Because CNN/Turner had gone out there early in the C-band, there are a lot of C-band cable dishes looking at those satellites in analog. To go to digital, you have to convert with all new digital decoders [for every receive site CNN must reach], and that ain't cheap.[7]

## Back to Basics

The history of CNN parallels the history of much of modern mass communication technology. CNN opened itself up to becoming a laboratory for the practical application of whatever was technologically current, whether in distribution, in newsgathering, or in news processing. As is the case with any beta-phase testing, some of CNN's efforts have been successful; some have not.

The availability of domestic satellites in 1976, when Ted Turner wanted to establish a national presence for his Atlanta-based television station, was a bit of good timing that has been seen to work for Turner Broadcasting time and again as new satellite capabilities emerged in the United States, Asia, Latin America, and Europe. From a technological standpoint, satellites provide an illustration of the rapid growth and internationalization of CNN.

---

6 Tauber, interview (August 1996).

7 Ibid.

In *Covering the World: International Television News Services*, Lewis Friedland described how financial necessity drove the struggling CNN network to use affiliate stations as primary newsgathering resources.

CNN offered its service via satellite in exchange for their video. By giving away its own product, CNN rapidly built up an affiliate network that, in breadth, rivaled that of the Big Three [U.S. broadcast networks]. By 1982, CNN had reciprocity agreements with about 125 local [U.S.] broadcasters.

The same principle was applied to international affiliates. CNN's foreign editor approached both public and commercial networks of other nations to exchange video on a story-by-story basis. Virtually none of the broadcasters outside of the United States had ever heard of CNN. But as these relationships were built over CNN's first years, an international network of affiliates gradually fell into place. . . . CNN was building the first international television news cooperative brick by brick.

Perhaps most important, CNN was committed to going live with breaking stories as often as possible. CNN was predisposed to live television for two reasons. Most of its news managers, on-air talent, and producers were products of local stations and had come of age with local televisioin in the 1970s, the heyday of live local "action" news. . . . The second reason was economic. Once CNN had paid for satellite time, the blocks might as well be filled with live television.[8]

Friedland noted the extraordinary impact of instantaneous news, reported in real time, directly from the site of events. According to Friedland, the first instance in which CNN was no longer just reporting events but shaping those events and even becoming part of them was triggered by its coverage of the Beijing Spring of 1989, which came to be known as the Tienanmen Square Massacre. "The China story also marked the first time a major breaking

---

[8] Lewis Friedland, *Covering the World: International Television News Services* (New York: Twentieth Century Fund, 1992): 16-17.

story was covered 24 hours a day for a worldwide television audience," observed Friedland.[9]

Satellites are not the only tools in the CNN work bag. If history is a guide, CNN will strive to utilize whatever means are available to the network to speed up the gathering and distribution of news. The telephone is probably the most frequently used of all telecommunications devices. It is more universally available and much cheaper than buying satellite time. The telephone is used to target and set up story coverage and, increasingly, it is used by CNN as the way to get live updates from the field without time-consuming and costly setups.

"Phoners," or "beepers" as they are more frequently called in broadcast news, function as real-time audio conferences between reporters and anchors, which usually incorporate an on-screen map of the area being discussed, a picture of the correspondent or newsmaker, and sometimes archival footage. According to one staffer on the International Desk, "Whenever news breaks, the first thing we're trying to do is get someone on the phone to explain or eyewitness it."[10] Beepers are used more and more by the *World Report* unit as well, as a way of bringing the contributors' local perspectives to the audience in a timely fashion and for relatively little money. "You have to be very creative if you want breaking news. Like [with today's] events in Russia, the quickest way to get [a report] is to get it by phone," according to Assignment Editor Andrew Henstock of the *World Report* unit.[11]

The decision in 1996 to take the *World Report* program to a live format reflected a desire on the part of the show's staff to make it more time-sensitive, remembered CNN Executive Vice President Bob Furnad.

> After the assassination [of Yitzhak Rabin] in Israel, Ralph [Wenge, Executive Producer for *World Report*, who also serves as anchor] did a live show. He felt it was incumbent on him to do a live show because that story was in such

---

[9] Ibid., 2, 4.

[10] Eli Flournoy (assignment editor, CNN International Desk), interview (January 1997).

[11] Andrew Henstock (assignment editor, *World Report*), interview (August 1996).

flux. Because the nature of *World Report* had changed from being a feature show to being a combination of hard news and feature news, clearly he needed to be live, to be as current as he could be on the story. After that experience, he came back and asked if we couldn't accommodate that show being done live on a weekly basis. So that portion of the show that deals with today's news can be live, can be current, can be immediate. Live satellites still are not possible but certainly live phone calls are. To help us be on the edge, to give the show that combination of today's news as fresh as it can be and of course feature material as well. That gives the show a whole new dynamic. I think any show that is live feels different. It feels different to the audience.[12]

To deliver live video as well as audio from the field by means of telephone technology has never worked particularly well. The reason is that ordinary telephone circuits do not have sufficient bandwidth to handle the additional information required for transmitting broadcast-quality television pictures. Nevertheless, two techniques using telephone lines to transmit pictures have been tried by CNN. The first was a transportable device that permitted video-audio transmission, either live or as store-and-forward images, by means of a digital dial-up access to the IN-MARSAT satellite. This sytem can deliver broadcast-quality full-motion pictures, but not in real-time.

According to Tauber, this store-and-forward transmission system was used by CNN in an interview from Baghdad with the Iraqi government's spokesman, Tariq Aziz, in 1996. Tauber said it worked well, despite the fact that

> it takes a minute to send a second of video; it takes an hour to send a minute of video. So at INMARSAT rates of $16 per minute for high-speed data, this was the best way to handle the situation.[13]

The economy of the dial-up satellite device is especially evident when compared to the several-thousand-dollar price tag for a full satellite feed, if available, plus the heavy cost of bringing in one of

---

[12] Bob Furnad (executive vice president, CNN), interview (December 1996). The first live *World Report* Sunday show aired on November 5, 1995.

[13] Tauber, interview (August 1996).

the company's fly-away earth stations to feed the satellite transmission.

*government action increase tech*

✓ Integrated systems digital networks (ISDN)—higher capacity landlines installed by the telephone companies—also are being used by CNN to improve the audio quality of the beepers and to provide still-frame video images. ISDN lines have been ordered by several CNN bureaus around the world as a way of feeding audio-video without ordering expensive satellite time.

Those who are less familiar with the problems associated with underdeveloped telecommunication infrastructures perhaps will be surprised to learn that CNN frequently must rely on transportation to ship information around. Often this takes the form of air courier services but sometimes it is even more basic than that. News material that is not time-sensitive, like feature pieces and indepth reports, usually are shipped directly to Atlanta, or to London or Tokyo where CNN maintains permanent satellite leases and does not incur separate feed charges.

*World Report* stories normally arrive in Atlanta by some form of air transportation. Kim Norgaard retraced the path a *World Report* package had to travel, even within recent years, to get from Africa to Atlanta.

> Since CNN does not pay for the shipment of reports to Atlanta [from *World Report* contributors] it is always a creative struggle for some contributors who are financially strapped to get their reports to us. Nigerian TV was such a case. I established contact with Yusuf Jibo who was very eager to send reports but naturally did not have the budget to ship by courier which would cost a couple of hundred U.S. dollars per shipment . . . so instead he came up with a novel idea. Yusuf had a friend out at the Lagos airport who was familiar with all the pilots. He devised a scheme which as crazy as it sounds actually worked. Yusuf would hand the tape off to one of the pilots flying for Nigerian airlines traveling to New York.
>
> I would receive a call from Yusuf with the flight number, arrival time and name of the pilot who had our package. Then, I would call our courier in New York who would meet the pilot and ship or FedEx our tape on to Atlanta. The scheme was just so bizarre, not to mention the se-

curity breach in having pilots hand-carrying anonymous packages, that it actually worked.

Then there was that Friday afternoon when Yusuf called telling me it was on such and such a flight being hand carried by Captain Bob. Captain Bob had delivered tapes for us before so I had no reason to be worried. However, the next morning I received a call from the courier who was at the airport but could not find Captain Bob. So began days of phone calls to Yusuf in Lagos. "What's the rest of his name? Where can I reach him?" Calls were placed to Nigerian airlines in the U.S., to the airport baggage claim, but all in vain. All I knew was that a certain Captain Bob had my tape somewhere. I wrote the package off and asked Yusuf to resend it.

The following Thursday I received a collect call from Seattle for Mr. Kim from Captain Bob. At first I thought it was a joke. No, it was our captain with the following explanation. He had arrived in New York but was in such a hurry to go on vacation that he did not have time to meet the courier and instead took it with him on vacation. He was calling me from Seattle to let me know that I could pick the tape up. Now, whenever there is a tape missing in transit the joke always resurfaces: "I'm sure Captain Bob has it."[14]

Gitana Lapinskaite was an anchor with the Lithuanian state television station on January 13, 1991, when Soviet President Mikhail Gorbachev sent troops back into Lithuania to reverse the country's declaration of independence from the Soviet Union. She was on the air live and reporting as the Soviet tanks approached, killing 14 and wounding 400 of the Lithuanians who had encircled the television tower in Vilnius.

In the days that followed, Lapinskaite and her television colleagues moved to the national Parliament building, which had not been occupied, and to Kaunas, the second largest city, to keep a broadcast signal going out to the Lithuanian people, who on the night of 'bloody Sunday' had begged her "Stay on the air. So long as we can hear you, we will know that we are still free."[15]

---

[14] Kim Norgaard (assignment editor, CNN International Desk), interview (October 1996).

[15] Ibid.

Lapinskaite recalled that her news director came to her with the request that she take a crew and begin preparing stories for airing on the CNN *World Report*. He told her that

> "With the CNN screen we can say to the world that we are not Russian and that we have absolutely no other nationality than Lithuanian, that we are still independent." I thought, "This cannot be. It cannot be that a country such as Lithuania can send a report to America and they will show it to the world, unedited without any censorship." For us, it was a little bit strange psychologically.[16]

The news director invited her to a planning meeting.

> I was afraid my English was bad. Maybe people will not understand and they will show for the whole world my language. He began to persuade me. He said "We will show the pictures. It doesn't matter too much if they only understand you a little." So I said, "OK, I can try."

She then took the television crew, using cameras and the limited portable gear the staff had smuggled out of the television station before the Soviet troops reduced it to rubble, and started preparing weekly stories about Lithuania for airing on *World Report*. Aside from the expected production problems, centering around a scarcity of videotape stock and only minimal editing capabilities in the regional station in Kaunas, a major problem developed in figuring out how to get the stories from behind the Iron Curtain to CNN in Atlanta. In the end, Lapinskaite found she had no choice but to send the tapes by way of Moscow.

> We were sending [them] with the diplomatic mail to some people I even don't know, to Lithuanian people we had connections with in Moscow. But it wasn't official. They were to take the tape and go straight to the CNN bureau in Moscow. But I made a mistake. I wrote in English and Lithuanian. Two of my reports were lost. I kept calling the CNN Moscow bureau. They then told me I was supposed to write only in Russian on the envelope.[17]

---

[16] Gitana Lapinskaite (Lithuanian State Television), interview (September 1996).

[17] Ibid.

Even today in Russia, as in numerous other places in the world, the whole "logistics thing" — as *World Report* assignment editor, Andrew Henstock, calls it — is no small task:

> Right in the middle of the Russian elections, we in *World Report* decided to do a two-hour special on Russia. The CNN bureau people were in a constrained workspace there in the Kapinski Hotel in Moscow. Already people were screaming at them from every conceivable direction and here I come phoning up: "By the way, this person or that person is going to be dropping by. We would really appreciate it if we could have the satellite between this time and that time." We try to work out the best ways to deliver a package. A lot of our stuff goes through London. Palestinian Broadcasting takes its packages around to the Jerusalem bureau. We've got a new contributor in Mongolia. They haven't got money to feed something to us. So we have to work out the cheapest way possible for them to deliver it. We worked out a way of sending it to the Beijing bureau so that when Beijing was going to send something to us, they would throw that tape in there. It works the same way with India, when we get something from Doordarshan, they send it over to our [New] Delhi bureau. When Delhi has got something going to London, they will drop that Doordarshan tape in.[18]

## The Internet Challenge

The Internet is a global telecommunications network of local and regional networks accessible via personal computers and PC-like communication devices. The rapidly expanding number of Internet users, estimated at 40 million worldwide in 1996, convinced CNN to create the CNN Interactive unit to respond to the trend. By the end of 1996, CNN Interactive employed 130 people, up from a total of three people in August 1995. CNN Interactive sites average 12 million hits (visits by Internet cyberseekers) a day, second only to the Netscape site.[19] No one at CNN is prepared to predict the ultimate impact of the Internet on the news business

---

[18] Henstock (August 1996).

[19] Internal CNN memo (December 1996).

or CNN, but the network's managers acknowledge its importance, and are devoting capital and staff time to it.

Among the attractive features of this new technology are its global reach, real-time interactive communications, news-on-demand, and reasonably economical access. For the moment, the limited bandwidth of the telephone lines used to carry Internet data move audio, video, and heavily illustrated graphic packages slowly. The Internet's great asset, which worries governments and the news media alike, is that practically any individual or group any where in the world can set up an information site that can be visited by any others. Information can be accessed and exchanged without an intermediary and without regard to national boundaries.

The explosive growth of relatively inexpensive personal computers, connected to the Internet and fitted with very agile browsers, puts home users in near-instantaneous touch with news stories, convincingly told in audio, video, and print. But not everything on the Internet has passed through the filter of a professional editor.[20] But the ease and economy involved in posting information in cyberspace mean that anyone for any motive can "publish" news-like material and be guaranteed a potential global audience. These developments prompt journalistic concerns but they also signal a competitive threat of unknown scope for existing news players.

Although computer networks are not yet extensively used to move video-based television news around, the inauguration date is not far off. In fact, according to CNNI's Eason Jordan, it already shapes CNN's planning strategy.

> It's a huge part of our future. You are seeing a melding of pictures and text in an interactive format. It's the future of the business in many ways. We are going to move into a more news-on-demand environment, at least people will have that option. At the same time, there is always going to be a market for program services, like the program services we have today. More and more people want to get the news when they want it and get exactly the news they want when

---

[20] Major news services such as CNN apply the same editorial standard to their online services as to their print or broadcast services.

they want it. Sort of creating your own television newscast or newspaper or whatever. We intend to be the principal information provider for everybody. That means using every means possible to reach the consumer, to give the consumer what she or he wants when she or he wants it. And, especially, as the technological advances come about, you really are going at some point to say you want your own customized newscast and it will happen for you when you want it to happen. So it is a big big part of our business.[21]

The future of news on the Internet is unclear. There are many who think the established agencies and broadcasters run a major risk of eventually being by-passed in the context of the World Wide Web. Jordan said he expects the audience for television news to remain an important market for companies like CNN;

My firm belief is there is always going to be a place for program providers in addition to content providers. Some people will obtain their content directly from the source. Other people will want to have an intermediary who can help them bring it all together in a fashion that has solid journalistic standards behind it. Today and in the future peole will have the option of getting the information directly from the source or through a news organization that can try to bring some perspective and depth to the news of the day.[22]

Whatever the distribution media, CNN's future as an international news organization is tied into its brand name,

Brands as we have seen in Coca-Cola, Mercedes-Benz, brands such as those. You really have to work to maintain and build your brand on a global basis. We certainly intend to do that by insuring that we are providing or making available news content and news programming through as many distribution means as make sense to as many people as possible.[23]

---

[21] Eason Jordan (senior vice president, CNN), interview (August 1996).

[22] Jordan, interview (December 1996).

[23] Ibid.

Put another way, CNN's reputation as a reliable news source in the context of television should translate into lots of visitors to its Web site (CNN.com). According to Tiven,

> We ain't a bunch of dumb clucks down here in Atlanta. For a variety of reasons we've got a really good Web. The Web was entrusted to a bunch of crazy maniacal entrepreneurial types. They did a good job.[24]

The proof is that advertising revenues increased from the first year; projected figures for 1997 are even greater. CNN's Web site had an operating profit just one year after going on-line.[25]

Nevertheless, Furnad, the primary overseer for what gets onto CNN air, said he is worried about the directions some of these developments seem to be taking, and sees danger for the company and for the credibility of journalism. He pointed to an example of how the information on the Internet can be misleading when there is no reputable information provider checking the information;

> Pierre Salinger (former press secretary under U.S. President John Kennedy) picked up a weeks-old story off the Internet that was speculation about what caused the TWA 800 explosion. He got on the Internet and started talking about it as if it were fact. Horribly dangerous.[26]

Furnad may have been especially sensitive to this abuse because CNN had put Salinger on the air with the information widely available on the Internet.

> [The] danger is not in the future. That danger is now. People see something on a computer screen and take it as fact. Why? Because people are used to looking at a television screen and accepting what is presented on there from the news media as fact. Now they see this information that they are getting off the computer that looks similar and they accept it as fact. . . . The fear is that people will make

---

[24] Ken Tiven, interview (December 1996).

[25] Scott Woelfel (vice president, CNN Interactive), interview (September 1996).

[26] Furnad, interview with Paolo Ghilardi (December 1996).

life-changing decisions based on information that could be horribly wrong.[27]

## Global Concerns

The president of the U.N. General Assembly, Razali Ismail of Malaysia, told broadcasters and government officials attending the United Nations World Television Forum[28] that globalization of communications and information technologies was glossing over some of the deeper implications of the communication revolution, particularly as they affect the poor, the voiceless, the young, and the marginalized.

> There is no doubting the growth and influence of electronic, satellite and information technology is astonishing. But its impact poses one of the biggest political and ethical issues of our time. Although many sectors of society benefit from this technology, we are also aware that those without access to it are further marginalized. Are we to enter the twenty-first century where every citizen in the North has a personal computer and television, but women in Africa still have to walk 30 miles to fetch potable water?[29]

He noted that only 83 percent of Latin American households have television sets. And television sets are even less common in Asia and Africa, with 64 percent of Asian households and 21 percent of African households served. While more than 11.6 percent of North American households can boast of Internet access, in Western Europe 2.7 percent of homes are connected. In developing countries, Asia leads with 0.8 percent of households having Internet access, with Africa and Latin America behind at 0.03 percent.[30]

---

[27] Ibid.

[28] Ted Turner gave the luncheon speech at the forum. New York City (22 November 1996).

[29] Ibid.

[30] Murtaza Mandli, "U.N. Chief Warns of North-South Technology Gap," Inter Press Service (22 November 1996).

Perhaps one of the greatest ironies of the "global village" is the growing and persistent phenomenon of exclusion, where individuals are simultaneously connected to the world by way of fibre optic cables and via satellite transmissions, but suffer from a pervasive loss and alienation from community values. . . . Information technology that spans the globe can concentrate ownership, limit access, homogenize content and pit freedom of expression against certain minimum standards. Therein lies our dilemma and our challenge.[31]

Ted Turner used his invitation to this same forum to air his views on several matters, the best received being his rebuke of the United States for exercising its veto powers to deny Boutros Boutros-Ghali's re-appointment as Secretary General. With Boutros-Ghali present, Turner asked, "Who is the United States to stand alone against the re-election of this good man here?"[32] He added, "Even England voted to re-elect this man and England always does what the United States asks them to do."[33]

Similarly, Turner chastised his country for failing to pay its debts. He asked the United States to pay up. "You owe the money, you pay it." He said he had considered buying the debt himself, estimated at $1.4 billion, "but I thought it would be a grandstand play and I would be criticized for doing it."[34]

Finally, Turner turned to his main topic: an appeal to the United Nations to help insure that whatever systems of mass media distribution and exchange were adopted as global standards were open to participation to all. The issue Turner raised was fundamentally one of technology and monopoly, according to David Usborne, writing in the *Independent*;

The liberalisation of the communications industry in the U.S., completed earlier this year, has unleashed forces that

---

31 Razali Ismail, speech (22 November 1996).

32 "Turner Slams Murdoch in Address to U.N. Panel," *Daily Variety* (25 November 1996): 14.

33 Anthony Goodman, "Ted Turner Blasts U.S. Veto, Rival Murdoch," Reuters Financial Service (22 November 1996).

34 "Turner Slams Murdoch in Address to U.N. Panel," 14.

*— competiton*

are transforming the landscape in America and worldwide. Most significant has been the rush of mergers and combina- tions, among them the $19 billion marriage of Walt Disney and ABC television last year, Mr. [Rupert] Murdoch's ac- quisition for $2.8 billion of New World Communications and its string of US TV stations this year and, of course, Time Warner's deal with Turner.

Usborne noted that the deal has made Time Warner–TBS argua- bly the most powerful media corporation on the planet.

The prospect of a world in which every household will de- pend on a single cable supplied by a single company for telephone, television, banking, shopping, Internet and who knows what new superhighway treats, has convinced every player that only the biggest, the most global, the most multi- media and the richest have a hope of survival. Only by dominating a lot of homes and a lot of media can you stay in the game.[35]

Usborne said this is generating an industry of elephants, each with enormous power. Concern is growing that this process is restricting real choice, not broadening it as the deregulators promised.[36]

Perhaps the only way to understand the impact of technol- ogy's push is within the context of competitive market forces. This point was crystalized in the aftermath of CNN's *live*, tech- nology-enabled Gulf War coverage. According to Mark Rudolph, the London-based director of CNN International Sales Limited,

The war compressed about 10 years of our development into about six months. The biggest change from [1990] to [1991] is our awareness level has moved from about 15 per- cent to 85 percent. There's virtually no one around anymore who doesn't know what CNN is.[37]

---

[35] David Usborne, "Murdoch Meets His Match; Ted Turner, Founder of CNN, is Taking Him On in New York," *Independent* (24 November 1996): 15.

[36] Ibid.

[37] Quoted in Janet Stilson, "CNN Steps Up Global Push in Persian Gulf War's Wake; Cable News Network to Open Far-flung News Bureaus after Covering Persian Gulf War," *Multichannel News* (29 July 1991): 3.

MOST OF THE COMPANIES *that are trying to enter markets [such as India, China, Indonesia] are public companies and can only afford to lose so much money. These are very difficult markets to enter because of the economics, the huge amount of capital that needs to be deployed for a long time before there is a payback. I don't think anyone knows how to conquer Asia and make money. We are all out there trying. We are probably losing the least amount of all the major players involved. Murdoch's News Corp. is losing hundreds of millions of dollars. GE/NBC probably 60 to 100 [million dollars]. . . . You are out there and you don't know why and you don't know what the results are going to be. You don't know the plan on how to get to be positive. A certain amount of caution is needed as these markets are being approached. The same pragmatism that made us highly successful when we saw the solution makes us slightly cautious [when we don't]. Our competitors are always trying to follow us into the fray and maybe we have led them down the wrong path. . . . I don't know that anybody can tell you they have an absolutely solid business plan on how they are going to succeed and make money. That's scary.*

Terry McGuirk*
Chairman, President, and CEO of TBS

---

* Interview (January 1997).

# 6

# The Pull of the Market

*I had just arrived at CNNI. I was sitting at lunch [with those attending the 1996* World Report *Contributors Conference] and it suddenly clicked. There is more to this than meets the eye. This is smart.*[1]

"CNN is facing competitive challenges in the U.S. and around the world. CNN is gearing up for war. [Even so,] these are fun, exciting and challenging times at CNN," Eason Jordan told journalists at the May 1996 *World Report* Contributors Conference in Atlanta as he introduced Chris Cramer, recently recruited away from the BBC to become a CNN International vice president;

> All great news organizations are led by strong, experienced and savvy individuals. Chris Cramer is a 25-year veteran of the BBC who grew up to be head of newsgathering. In my many years at CNN I have never known a more ferocious competitor.[2]

Cramer was hired in 1996 specifically to help develop and implement a strategy for internationalizing CNN. He did not waste time putting his stamp on the company. By July 1996 he had produced *CNNI–Beyond 2000*, a concept paper distributed to his fellow members of CNN's Executive Committee for discussion. He also had circulated the draft to the staff of CNN International,

---

[1] Chris Cramer (vice president, CNN International), interview (December 1996).

[2] Ibid. See Charles Haddad, "CNN Hires No. 2 Man from BBC," *Atlanta Constitution* (8 February 1996): E1.

where he serves as managing editor. In the draft, Cramer tried to set the tone for what lay ahead:

> CNNI is now producing about 70 percent original pro-gramming during the week, an average of 60 percent across the full seven days. We are now ready to move into the next phase of CNNI's development. To move to full maturity in a way which will continue to keep us well ahead of what-ever opposition we may face.[3]

It is appropriate to assess where the channel now is, he wrote, and to improve it the company needs to keep focused on CNNI's basic strategy. That strategy is:

- To continue to be the foremost provider of inter-national news for the World.

- To continue to attract the key opinion formers in all markets.

- To be the channel where news is first broken, re-ported and analyzed.

- To provide varied and innovative programming for a range of viewers around the World who take news and public affairs seriously. CNNI will be fresh and engaging with the best anchors and drawing upon the best newsgathering correspon-dents in the business.

- The channel will schedule the best of CNN and is committed to providing an appropriate service of news from America as well as the rest of the World.

- CNNI will develop new program formats and lengths to complement its existing services.

- It will invite viewer participation and, where ap-propriate, will respond to the views of its audi-ence.

---

[3] *CNNI–Beyond 2000* (July 1996).

- When possible CNNI will regionalize its news services to provide more focus and relevance.

- It will seek to develop specific programming for the Asia, Europe and Latin markets.[4]

By the end of 1996, Chris Cramer and the CNNI staff were well along in the implementation of a three-year plan for changes in the program schedule and content. "CNN International has for the last 11 years made an extremely good living. Indeed, for many of those years in a monopolistic situation without competition. That is absolutely not the case now," Cramer acknowledged. He said CNN has a variety of competitors. The one he will focus on is BBC World, because it is closest to CNN in terms of news product, but there are NBC's various international channels, Asia Business News, Euronews and other services akin to what CNN does.

"If you focus on our two most particular markets, i.e., Europe, which includes Africa, and Asia, which includes Australia and New Zealand, then you've got two quite distinct types of battle-grounds there," Cramer said.

> What will happen in 1997 and what Time Warner and Ted Turner have signed on to, as far as CNN International is concerned, is a three-year strategy. The company has accepted a strategy, which I have put together with Eason Jordan, which says: if we are to maintain our carriage and influence in Europe and develop our carriage and influence in Asia, we've got to regionalize.

> What we've now got to do is to start producing tailored programming for individual regions. That will mean in 1997 we will start to produce back-to-back parallel programming, part of it out of Atlanta, part of it out of a region like Europe and back into that region, out of a region like Asia and back into Asia. At the same time on the same hour of the same day, you will have a different news program going to the rest of the world out of Atlanta.[5]

---

[4] Ibid.

[5] Cramer, interview (December 1996).

He noted that CNNI currently transmits globally on 15 satel-lites using four distinct regional feeds. North America is one of these ("a small one, influential, but not a revenue driver") deliv-ered to home viewers on direct satellite. Latin America, currently an important marketplace for CNN, after March 1997 will also have a 24-hour Spanish language channel, so there will be two types of CNN service going into Latin America: the English CNNI version and the new one, CNN en Español.

> At any given time of day, we have four separate program-ming streams of CNNI going out. There is different ad in-ventory and some different programming but primarily it is the same spine.

> That will all change in 1997. In 1997, we will start moving our programming around, a little bit like coconut shells. We will start to produce time-specific and regionally-specific programming. Why are we doing that? No note of desperation here, it's because we recognize, and indeed the audience is telling us, whereas they value and have a great deal of affection for the way CNN covers international news, they want it to be more regionalized.

> Not localized. We don't rule out doing some vernacu-lar channels either as co-ventures like we do in Germany[6] now or as translations like we do in parts of Japan. But we are not in the business of competing with the local broad-caster. That is not our job and they would do it better than we anyway. What we do believe we are in the business of is providing an intelligent international news service, which in '97, '98 and '99 we will start to dramatically tailor our pro-gramming to a regional perspective, and that's the big change in CNNI, that's the hook we think will maintain our position as the market leader.[7]

During 1996, several news programs were dropped from CNNI's schedule, including the U.S.-oriented *Crossfire*, *Inside Politics*, and *Business Day*. In their place, CNNI showcased se-lected material from the new business channel, CNN*fn*, and

---

[6] In 1992, CNN bought into the Berlin-based n-TV, part of an effort to co-venture with vernacular services. In 1994, CNN pulled out of its Russian language ven-ture in Moscow, TV6.

[7] *CNNI–Beyond 2000.*

added CNN-produced shows such as *Late Edition, Pro Golf Weekly,* and *Showbiz This Week,* thought to have appeal for the international audience. Two new CNNI-produced shows were introduced: *Insight* with Jonathan Mann and *Q&A* with Riz Khan. Summary news programs tailored to regions, such as *World News Europe, World News Asia, World News Americas, Inside Asia, American Edition,* and *Inside Africa,* were in the process of being implemented.

The CNNI approach to regional weather was modified and GMT (Greenwich Mean Time) reinstated as a program reference. In 1996, CNNI commissioned and aired its first independent production, "Return to the Lions Den," charting Terry Anderson's return to Beirut for the first time since his release in 1991.[8] Cramer said his goal is to

> continue to produce "landmark" programming — programs the audience positively want to tune in for, to make an appointment with. I want to vary the service on CNNI. To give it more light and shade.[9]

Eason Jordan, who had a strong hand in internationalizing CNN and now holds administrative responsibility for international coverage and international relations, noted that while CNN International is still a young network, it has undergone some radical changes in 11 years, the most dramatic of which occurred in 1996. The hiring of Cramer was one of those changes in 1996, one that promises even more change in the coming years "as we rise to the challenge of an intensely competitive marketplace which did not exist in the early years of CNN and CNNI," according to Jordan.

> There are a lot of things we must do — and will do — to not only maintain but widen the competitive lead we have. One of the things we are doing . . . is regionalization. [We are] embarking down a path of simultanously sending out separately-produced program strands to separate parts of the world. So while Asia might wake up to programming

---

[8] Cramer, with Sid Harris, wrote *Hostage* (London: J. Clare Books, 1982), a firsthand account of the 1980 siege of the U.S. Embassy in Iran, in which he was held hostage.

[9] *CNNI–Beyond 2000.*

presented from Asia for Asians, at that same time Europe, Africa, Latin America, and the Middle East will perhaps be seeing different programming . . . world news will always be the backbone of the CNN service, U.S. news as a part of that will always be prominent, but this is a global service with an international perspective. What we want to do is heighten the relevance of the service.[10]

Jordan used *Crossfire* to illustrate why CNN opted to take some of the shows that are popular in the United States off the international service.

First of all, the only part of the world that was seeing it was Asia. Because at that time to Latin America we were airing a Spanish program and, at that time to Europe it was the middle of the night, and in Central Europe it was airing at 2:30 in the morning, so we had to think about our Asia audience. Even in the United States *Crossfire* would not fly in a breakfast television timeslot. Think about the time difference, and think about the timeliness of the program. You can't just hold the program for 12 to 14 hours. It is not always going to be timely because it is a very topical program.

The concern we had was, first of all, is *Crossfire* proper wake-up breakfast TV? I would venture there is no country in the world where you can argue [that] it is. Secondly, while *Crossfire* is a terrific program for Americans, it has a machine-gun, rapid-fire manner to it that in many cultures is just inappropriate. It just doesn't work. Thirdly, the program understandably, being a Washington-based largely political program, is very, very U.S.-centric. Whereas it is wholly approriate for the domestic market and while the world certainly cares about what happens in the United States, if you combine those three factors, it just seemed to be inappropriate for CNNI. Maybe that is an incorrect decision but it is one we believe is right and we are going forward without it.[11]

---

[10] Eason Jordan (senior vice president, CNN), interview (December 1996).

[11] Jordan, interview (August 1996).

In addressing the new CNNI strategy, he noted that

> in select countries you may see us introducing some national content, although at no time do we intend to challenge national broadcasters. We see ourselves as a complementary service to the existing national broadcasters. . . . We have this large ownership of n-TV in Germany, which is a national network in German, but it could be that at some point we will insert into CNN International some product from the country where the signal is being seen. It has not happened yet but it may happen in the next year or so.[12]

## The Turner Culture

*globalization — merger*

In October 1996, shareholders of Time Warner Inc. and Turner Broadcasting System Inc. approved a merger of the two companies into a single $6.5 billion organization. Gerald R. Levin, Time Warner chairman, became chairman of the new company; TBS chairman Ted Turner became vice chairman. Work was begun to rationalize management structures and to integrate the assets of the two companies, which include cable operations, professional sports teams, extensive film and animation libraries, entertainment and news production capabilities and facilities, and international TV syndication and distribution services.

Terry McGuirk was appointed chairman, president, and CEO of Turner Broadcasting System — titles held by his boss, Ted Turner, before Turner became vice chairman of Time Warner. The 45-year-old McGuirk started with the Turner organization in 1972, and has seen it grow from 30 employees to more than 8000. According to McGuirk, Time Warner–TBS is now the largest player in the cable universe; he predicts that the Turner networks have the largest growth potential of any of the businesses Time Warner is in.[13]

---

[12] Ibid.

[13] Diane Mermigas, "Time Warner-Turner Merger's First Effect Likely Seen Overseas," *Electronic Media* (7 October 1996): 46.

In a December 1996 media trade magazine interview about the Turner business philosophy, McGuirk commented that Jerry Levin was

> very smart in allowing this culture to continue to prosper and understanding its unique nature. Time Warner has done all the right things to get the maximum out of this company.[14]

In an interview for this book, McGuirk reflected on the Turner culture:

> If you think back to the origins of the company, in the early 70s we were a very small company trying to break into a very big broadcast and communciations world that didn't look kindly on newcomers trying to take a piece of the pie. To grow from this undercapitalized situation to today it took a tremendous amount of luck, smarts, leadership by Ted, and most importantly we couldn't make many mistakes. For every two or three forward steps we took one or two back; we were not sufficiently well-capitalized.[15]

McGuirk was reminded that the company had taken on some financially and even politically risky projects, in which the probability of failure would seem quite high—projects such as the Goodwill Games and the *World Report*. Each involved international politics, which not only might offend the U.S. government and turn off the American viewing public, but also appeared at the time to offer little prospect of helping the network make money.

> Not making money directly off of a singular event or project is part of the mystery of this place. We are all long-term thinkers here. We have all been trained at the management level of this company to build assets and not to be focused on immediate P&L [profit and loss] goals. That's surely the way Ted has always thought. Building value. If something brought value, in his mind, over a longer period of time, we would have no problem committing to it, because he knew that it logically would produce results maybe just beyond the normal three-to-five-year timeline for long-range plans

---

[14] Lee Hall, "The Man Behind the Man," *Electronic Media* (9 December 1996): 38.

[15] Terry McGuirk (CEO/president, TBS), interview (January 1997).

that most people have. That's the way this company has succeeded. The ultimate successful goals are really what we focus on, and the many intermediate steps we in this company must take to get there.

Doing CNN didn't make a lot of sense for a small company like ourselves, but when you just look at the opportunity . . . everytime [Ted Turner] added up the obvious in the '79 to '80 time-period before we launched, it just kept coming up that this works, in his computer, yet it looked like it couldn't work to most naysayers. But they weren't looking at the same thing. Ted is a very pragmatic businessman. Most of the people who are making the decisions in this company are trained that way, but because we think longer-term, it looks riskier.[16]    🠖 policy

As for *World Report* specifically, he noted:

We are not so insular as to believe that only news in the United States makes sense. We want to be connected to every corner of the world. In fact, that's a lot of the magic of what we have created. We do connect to every point in the world and have reciprocal relationships and do very good business in all these places. Influence isn't always a profit-oriented phenomenon. Having good relationships with people who can't necessarily afford to pay for your service is still a good thing. This *World Report*, I think, provides a very good service and brings CNN to places it might not get to. One of the basic instincts in business is to make friends with people you are doing business with. We believe very strongly in that. . . . We *are* trying to bring these broadcasters into the family and create a much smaller world. It is all of what is wrapped up in the successful nature of this company.[17]

*World Report's* founding executive producer, Stuart Loory, remembered that the program almost immediately benefited Turner's broadcasting companies;

The earliest impact it had internationally was . . . the impact on TBS' marketing internationally. The way I know about that is that Bob Ross at that time was the head of the TBS'

---

[16] Ibid.

[17] Ibid.

operation in Europe. He discovered in the first year or two years of the *World Report* that people were coming to see him at the two big trade shows for television. . . . Very often, he was being asked about the CNN *World Report*. As a result of that, he asked me to come to those meetings and I went for two or three years, twice a year, to the meetings because people wanted to talk to somebody from CNN *World Report*. It was wonderful and I was able to make a speech about the program and at the same time Turner International was able to get some benefits out of the fact that we had the CNN *World Report* representative there who could talk of the program and helped to show people how serious Turner was about its international relations and about international penetration.[18]

CNNI's Jordan said he has no doubt that Time Warner elected to keep the CNN organization intact because of Ted Turner's track record in the area of understanding markets. Turner has been a hands-on chairman and leader at TBS and is expected to continue as an active vice chairman at Time Warner, where he heads the television division which includes CNN. Jordan argued that Time Warner recognizes that CNN is a dynamic, innovative, and hard-charging news organization "growing by leaps and bounds, even 16 years after its creation."[19]

Cramer, who had had plenty of opportunity to observe the Turner culture from afar during his years at the BBC, said he finds the Turner/CNN culture "extremely teamly;"

The notion of team-working is real here, very very inclusive, even for outsiders like myself. There is a desire here for you to succeed, not fail, and I come from a culture where they like you to fail. I may be naive, but I see this as fact. Very much an information-sharing culture, not an information-is-power culture. The notion of failure does not exist. I am not sure it is in their dictionary.[20]

---

[18] Stuart Loory (former executive producer, *World Report*), interview (October 1996).

[19] Jordan, interview (December 1996).

[20] Cramer, interview (December 1996).

CNN has earned the right to be left alone by Time Warner, according to Cramer. "What is very clear is that Time Warner sees CNN, the CNN grouping, as the crown jewels. Time Warner has many other assets but they have always seen CNN as the crown jewels," according to Cramer. He said that the idea of the "CNN family" is a reflection of Turner's commitment to holding it together, a view that is shared throughout the company.

> There is a lot of Atlanta and a lot of the south in CNN, [possibly] the result of Ted [Turner] and Tom [Johnson]. My own personal impression of Atlanta in the first few weeks was that I'd never before seen people jog at 5:30 in the morning in the pitch dark. It says a lot about Atlanta. It certainly says a lot about the South.[21]

The fact that CNN's top managers have given Cramer the power to make changes says much about the company, according to Cramer;

> Hiring someone at my level from outside the company takes a very mature organization. They've given me the freedom to hire from wherever I wanted to hire around the world. And I have done that. I've hired a half-dozen—more than that—extremely able executives and on-the-screen anchors, and not from CNN and not from America. So when they talk international, they *mean* international. They do have a culture of promotion from within, but they will buy in whatever they need to keep ahead.[22]

Cramer pointed to the company's investment in the CNN Interactive project as an example;

> I am not sure they know where it is going. They just know that it is important and they know that they need to be out in front. That's why a year ago it had four people and now it's got, what, a hundred and thirty? And it's already making money. There is a passion, not so much to be on the leading edge of the envelope, but even further than that, wherever that is, beyond the window.[23]

---

[21] Ibid.

[22] Ibid.

[23] Ibid.

Asked whether Turner's social philosophy of doing business by doing good was an effective approach to the international news business, Cramer remembered that

> Before I came to CNN, it had been pointed out to me that there was a belief within the organization that television could be a force for good, not evil. For a grand English skeptic, that is a curious view. When you get here, you know that they mean it. And interestingly you start to share it. They do believe that contacts and relationships and affiliations are critically important in being successful. They foster and nourish, indeed they cherish, those relationships every day of the week. But the catalyst for it is not money-making. It is the belief that it is right, the belief that it is also incredibly competitive. In that, we come back to *World Report*, don't we? [CNN has] the most affiliations of any broadcast organization in North America, indeed among all the news organizations in the world combined. And they have spent years working on it. They live and breathe it.[24]

## The Third Age of CNN

The *Financial Times* asked Tom Johnson, president and CEO of the CNN News Group, about the impact on CNN of increased competition in the international news business. Johnson described 1996 as the beginning of the Third Age of CNN. The First Age was the establishment of the 24-hour cable news service beginning in 1980. The Second Age began with CNN's coverage of the Gulf War in 1990. The Third Age begins with the emergence of real competition.[25]

In responding to that competition, Johnson called attention to CNNI strategies to regionalize its programming, to continue in its effort to make CNN less American and to move into important languages other than English. He noted the development of new networks such as the new Spanish language service CNN en Español, the CNN joint venture with *Sports Illustrated*, also a Time

---

[24] Ibid.

[25] "CNN Digs Its Claws In: Raymond Snoddy Meets CNN News Group Chairman Tom Johnson," *Financial Times* (9 December 1996): 19.

Warner company, to create CNN-SI, and expansion of the mostly domestic CNN Airport Network to international sites.

Johnson also pointed to some technological developments, such as CNN live on commercial aircraft via mobile satellite, up-to-the-minute CNN headline news on personal pagers, and the ventures into interactive TV and the Internet. "The test," said Johnson, "is do these projects work journalistically? Do they work operationally? And do they work financially?"[26]

David Clinch is an international assignment editor on the International Desk. As an international hire, he said he has given some thought to what is really international about CNNI, how the international service developed and why. "The essential point to think about is whether CNN became international accidentally or deliberately," he said.

> It seemed to me that it happened somewhat accidentally — due to the fact of satellite availability for distribution, and that international outlets were suddenly available that did not exist before. [CNN actually] went international before the service was itself international. It was successful even before it made an effort to internationalize itself. If this is so, you have got to assume it was successful for what it was, that is, an American network. CNN was an American news service, America-based, with an American point of view and style. CNN was successful internationally for exactly the same reason it was successful in the United States. It was news, it was information and it was 24-hours a day.[27]

Such a service perhaps would have been successful no matter where it originated, whether in Great Britain or Indonesia or anyplace else, according to Clinch. The important point was that it was a 24-hour service of news and information delivered where the audience was.

> Like the Beatles might not have been successful if the mass distribution of records had not happened at that time, the accident of Turner coming up with the idea of 24-hours of

---

[26] Tom Johnson (president, CNN), interview with Paolo Ghilari (November 1996).

[27] Ibid.

news was matched by the availablity of satellite and cable distribution in the United States.[28]

CNN was simply an extension of that, he said. And probably CNNI was begun following the same pattern.

> Then you come back to [the question], well, we have an international service, lots of people are watching us, are we making any money at this? The answer generally was no, because there was no international advertising market. There were some internationally advertised products, such as Coca-Cola, but no global advertising market. So there became a need, not from a programming but from a marketing point of view, to create a service that could be marketed. In a sense, the pressure came backwards. There was obviously a consciousness that you needed to be neutral in terms of reference to us as Americans. But the pressure, I believe, to become a separate international service was a marketing thing.[29]

Clinch said he sees the internationalizing of personnel, of program content and schedule on CNNI as a response to the demands of that new marketplace.

> CNN was paying out lots of money for [satellite] distribution. If you go to Hong Kong and asked local companies if they wanted to buy advertisements on CNN, they would logically ask, "How many people are watching?" CNN would say, "We don't know." Then, because the number of outlets grew, in hotels and on the local cable systems, CNN was able to go to them and say, "Look, you've got CNN on your service. Would you pay us for advertising?" Then they would say, "Yes, but we want more Asian news." Or "Yes, but you are too American." Or "Yes, but we prefer you do this and not that."[30]

---

[28] Ibid.

[29] Ibid.

[30] Ibid.

## International Sales and Marketing

Ask the CNN news staff and the CNN/TBS management to name the factors contributing to the company's ability to international-ize, and the former probably would de-emphasize the value of *World Report*, while management might over-emphasize it. Man-agement knows that *World Report* is sacred and protected ground for the ultimate boss, Ted Turner, which is one possible explana-tion for the difference. They are ready to give Turner's pet project credit, and may better recognize the value of the program from a marketing standpoint. *The Guardian*, for example, noted the benefit to the network when U.S. President Bill Clinton partici-pated in the *World Report's* first-ever *Global Forum* program, staged from the Carter Center in Atlanta as part of the 1994 Con-tributors Conference;

> Presented as a town meeting with the planet, President Clinton spent 90 minutes answering questions from journal-ists in Sarajevo and Seoul, Johannesburg and Jerusalem. . . . A triumph of English as the common tongue and of tech-nology, last night's global hook-up represented the heavy weapon in CNN's drive to beat off its BBC, Sky-TV and other competitors and assert its dominance of the world media market. . . . And in Bill Clinton, a president who be-lieves that the soft power of U.S. trade and cultural influ-ence is as important as the military hardware of a super-power, CNN deployed its ultimate salesman last night.[31]

It is also true that, while *World Report* has helped CNN cover the news faster and more comprehensively than anyone else, and although *World Report* creates goodwill among local broadcasters and broadcast stations and opens doors to CNN coverage and the marketing of CNN/TBS products, *World Report* is a symbol. *World Report* represents an attitude, a culture of inclusion, openness and fair play that the company's managers want to project, and to market. This image, though fraught with difficulty in its imple-mentation, has a lot to do with Turner's international success.

---

[31] Martin Walker, "Nation Speaks Unto Nation — Via CNN," *The Guardian* (4 May 1994): 9.

Herein is the paradox reflected in reconciling capitalism and social responsibility, in being held accountable to shareholders for acceptable rates of return while going out of the way to give voice to those who haven't and may never have the means to buy the company's products. In the news business, which depends on public credibility as well as profitability, this conundrum is very real.

TBS has a close but delicate working relationship with the People's Republic of China. In 1996, a Chinese Long March rocket went awry, destroying an expensive Intelsat satellite and killing an undetermined number of people in the vicinity of the launch pad; some estimate that the casualties could be as high as several hundred. This story was reported on CNN only in very general terms because the news media could never get in to cover the event and the story could never be verified firsthand from either the western or Chinese sources present.[32] On the other hand, there is some speculation that a Chinese dissident sentenced to prison for expressing views unfavorable to the government is now freed because CNN and other news agencies so relentlessly covered the story, embarrassing the Chinese officials into responding to world pressure.

Indonesia, now with the fourth largest population in the world after China, India, and the U.S., is a prime market for CNN. In the mid-1990s, CNN moved its Southeast Asian bureau from Manila to Jakarta. Indonesia has liberal public satellite reception policies and a growing number of commercial broadcast stations that are candidates to air CNN material. On the other hand, Indonesia has highly repressive policies toward its own press and brooks no criticism of government policy, and certainly not of the president or members of the first family, who control much of the nation's business, including the independent stations that were set up to provide alternatives to TVRI, the state broadcaster.

Yet, in late 1996, CNN and CNNI ran news features on the Nobel Peace Prize winners Bishop Carlos Ximenes Belo and the exiled Jose Ramos-Horta. Citizens of Indonesia, Belo and

---

[32] Eli Flournoy (assignment editor, CNN International Desk), interview (August 1996).

Ramos-Horta had been chosen "for their work toward a just and peaceful solution to the conflict in East Timor."[33] Speaking in Hamburg, Germany, Indonesian Foreign Minister Ali Alatas said he was "astounded the peace prize could be given to a political adventurist" and a statement issued by the Ministry of Foreign Affairs said

> Ramos-Horta was a key leader of the Fretlin, a radical po-
> litical group . . . which Bishop Belo himself publicly con-
> demned for the brutality of their brief rule. . . . Jose Ramos-
> Horta has yet to account for his complicity and responsibil-
> ity in that bloodbath.[34]

CNN managers have said the network is committed to cover-ing the news wherever it finds it, and that is a matter not to be confused with its friendly relations with particular countries or stations. Certainly, the company must walk a fine line to maintain cordial relationships and yet continue to report stories critically and objectively from whatever direction news appears. CNN's Tom Johnson addressed this topic in a press interview:

> CNN wants to avoid the problems experienced by the BBC
> in providing an Arabic TV service for the Saudi-backed
> Orbit Communications Group which collapsed earlier this
> year in mutual recriminations. CNN has rejected proposals
> from Saudi groups for a Middle East service because of po-
> tential political difficulties. If we can't go into a country and
> operate with independence, then we just won't do it.[35]

Johnson added that CNN is nonetheless allowed to report from North Korea and has plans to open a bureau in Havana, Cuba following approval from the U.S. government. In a presentation to the Media Studies Center forum at Columbia University in mid-December 1996, Eason Jordan told the group that

> Cuban officials say they're eager for us to move quickly to
> establish a bureau in Havana. CNN Havana bureau chief-
> designate Lucia Newman, Larry Register and I spent

---

[33] "Peace Prize: Belo OK, but Horta? No Way!" *News and Views of Indonesia*, Re-public of Indonesia, Directorate of Information (October 1996): 1-2.

[34] Ibid.

[35] "CNN Digs Its Claws In . . . ."

Monday to Wednesday on a scouting mission in Havana. We met foreign minister Robaina, parliament president Alarcon, Cuban TV president Roman and others in an effort to insure we'll be able to open the bureau at first opportunity. We can move ahead only if the U.S. Government approves our application for the bureau. Cuban officials say their decision to allow CNN to have a permanent presence first in Havana is unconditional. They say they'll never attempt to meddle in our reporting. They acknowledge the Cuban Government likely will be displeased with some of CNN's reporting from Cuba. Nevertheless, they say CNN's bureau will be welcome there as long as CNN's reporting is accurate and fair.[36]

In any story CNN reports, from whatever country, the staff tries to be fair and exercise good judgment, according to Rob Golden of the CNN International Desk.

It is true that sometimes we need to be more tactful, and careful in our approach. For example, an aggressive style by reporters may be fully acceptable in a place like Israel where the culture accepts or tolerates that sort of behavior. But journalists would have to take a more warmhearted approach in Arab countries — sitting for tea with interviewees, for example. Almost every country has its sensitivities. We try not to offend anyone. In India, for example, the government expressed its displeasure with a story we did which featured many cows roaming the streets of India. In their view, we did not approach the story with the proper respect for the Hindu religious symbols. We have been very sensitive to that ever since, and we will give the proper treatment to any such stories in the future.[37]

He said the decision to undertake stories that might offend a host country will always face scrutiny: Does the importance of the story outweigh whatever repercussions (i.e., being kicked out of the country) may result? These are case by case decisions,

---

[36] "The Future of Free Press in Cuba," the Columbia University Seminar on Communications and Society, Columbia University Media Studies Center (19 December 1996). See: http://www.mediastudies.org. The U.S. government gave its approval for the CNN bureau in February, 1997.

[37] Rob Golden (assignment editor, CNN International Desk), interview (December 1996).

according to Golden. But there have been surprisingly few retributions from governments over the years. In most cases, the governments, such as Saudi Arabia, which do not want CNN to report on stories in their country take *a pre-emptive* approach: they deny visas.

> As a matter of principle we will never knowingly do a "favorable" story on a country in order to curry favor with a particular government or official. All stories are reported based on news value, not to further the interests of CNN.[38]

Clinch also made a distinction between news that *costs* money versus news that *makes* money. There are not just political sensitivities but economic realities to be faced and decisions to be made.

> What goes on the [CNN] International air is a constantly moving target. On occasion, the pressure commercially will be: "Let's put O.J. Simpson on." That would not be editorial. That would not be because the world cared, though they did. It was because it would make us money. In the same sense, there is pressure to put things on the air that will make us no money at all, because it makes editorial sense. There are those of us on the International Desk who want to spend money on an event even though nobody cares about it. Like being able to stand on the border between Rwanda and Zaire and show how hundreds of thousands of people *live*, in such a way that the world changed. Not because of our coverage but because an international decision was made from available information that there was no need for a multi-national force. And many such choices are made every day which do not pay their way. You probably can't do it any other way.[39]

*Third.*

## The Rising Competition

Tom Johnson has said that CNN will be a better news service as the field of competitors gets more crowded.

---

[38] Ibid.

[39] David Clinch (assignment editor, CNN International Desk), interview (November 1996).

> ⌈We need the competition. We want the competition. It's
> what spurs us to keep ahead — that and the way the world
> leaders now come to us.[40]⌉

CNN managers are convinced that in the future their competitors in international news will not be the American "entertainment" networks (ABC, CBS, and NBC), but rather the companies that are trying to be global. CNN is a company whose main mission is news. CNN is news-driven, not program-driven, in that the assignment desk covers everything that is news wherever it appears in the world without regard to whether a particular show on a particular CNN network — on CNNI, CNN*fn*, CNN-SI, CNN en Español, CNN Newsroom or CNN Airport Network — will find a time slot for it. The Weekend Features unit of CNN does create a lot of program-driven work, and special programs are commissioned for a variety of purposes. But all producers have the option of picking and choosing from a rapidly updated list of stories (and raw footage) that includes everything from U.S. to Russian elections, from returning refugees in Kigali, Rwanda, to hostage-taking in Lima, Peru, from Dow Jones to the Thai stock market. The CNN news philosophy is: if it is important, it will be covered.

CNN executive vice president Ed Turner took umbrage when Sam Donaldson of ABC News remarked that the U.S. networks gave the 1996 Republican National Convention in San Diego, California, so little coverage because it looked more like an "infomercial than a news event,"

> annoying that some journalists and news executives seem to
> think it has to be entertaining to be news. . . . The subject of
> the governance of the country for the next four years is
> really important, even if personalities are well-behaved.[41]

He explained that CNN's extensive coverage "goes with the territory. Our colleagues [at ABC, CBS and NBC] are in another

---

[40] Johnson, quoted in Walker, 9. Walker wrote of the *Global Forum* and other discussions at the 1994 *World Report* Contributors Conference that were broadcast live on CNNI, featuring "world leaders, including Clinton, Rabin and Arafat, joining a global television hook-up as part of an orgy of self-promotion by the satellite channel."

[41] Ed Turner (executive vice president, CNN), quoted in Heather Fleming, "The No News Convention," *Broadcasting And Cable* 126 (19 August 1996): 8.

business—entertainment—and we're not."[42] Nonetheless, the American broadcast networks have not given up the turf entirely, and remain formidable competitors in the U.S. market. In related markets they are CN competitors abroad.

# NBC

MSNBC is a 24-hour cable and Internet news service[43] launched in July 1996 as a joint venture of NBC and Microsoft, the computer software company. A 10 M/byte ATM (multimedia) data line, supplied by the long-distance telephone carrier MCI, links the geographically dispersed news operation, drawing in the on-line production facilities in Redmond, Washington, NBC News in New York, various NBC News bureaus, and the cable headquarters in Secaucus, New Jersey.[44]

The network announced that it would have access to 20 million subscribers in the U.S. and Canada at launch. The service is intended to complement NBC broadcast and CNBC, begun in 1989 as the NBC-owned business news/talk cable channel reaching more than 58 million homes. According to Merrill Brown, managing editor for MSNBC Internet, the company plans to position its on-line component as a unique, stand-alone product that will become the Internet's daily news magazine drawing on material from NBC, CNBC, and MSNBC.[45]

"It is basically the first Internet news organization built from the bottom up with the Internet in mind," argued Brown.

> Its primary mission will be to do quick, topical delivery of breaking news. Aggressive use will be made of audio and

---

[42] Ibid.

[43] See http://www.msnbc.com.

[44] Ken Freed, "MSNBC Interactive Merges TV, Web," *TV Technology* (29 November 1996): 29.

[45] "MSNBC Aims to be 'Net News Mag," *Broadcasting & Cable* 126 (24 June 1996): 45.

eventually video content. In startup, MSNBC online is offered free to users. CNN is seen as its chief online rival.[46]

Mark Harrington, MSNBC vice president and general manager, said the service will be

> different from CNN and there is room for both. They've
> been at it for 15 years. With 60 million homes they have a
> different universe, but we have the strength of NBC News
> and its big-name talent as well as the Microsoft tie, which
> gives us an enormous step into the Internet world.[47]

To succeed, said Harrington, MSNBC must bring new viewers
to the service, not just take CNN viewers. The on-line connection
is designed to capitalize on that trend and drive viewers back and
forth between a company's broadcast, cable, and cyberspace outlets. NBC News Channel, the broadcast affiliate news cooperative,
will be a key supplier to MSNBC. MSNBC must pay a license fee
for this material. In addition, the cable channel will depend on
affiliates to produce packages and provide live shots with local
reporters.[48]

According to *Business Week's* Amy Cortese and Rob Hof,

> Microsoft and NBC . . . both concede that MSNBC is not
> likely to have an immediate payoff. Their goals are long-
> term. Microsoft hopes to build a bigger presence in the con-
> verging worlds of media and computers and expects that
> constant promotion on NBC and the MSNBC cable channel
> will drive customers to the MSNBC Interactive Web site. If
> significant numbers of viewers are Net cruisers, too, the
> joint venture may prove the viability of an advertising-
> driven Internet site. . . . For NBC, the MSNBC venture is a
> key step in expanding beyond its core *U.S.* broadcasting
> business. Since 1989, NBC has launched CNBC in the U.S.,
> Europe, and Asia, an NBC channel in Asia and NBC Super

---

[46] Ibid.

[47] Ibid.

[48] Steve McClellan and Rich Brown, "Cable News Prepares for War," *Broadcasting & Cable* 126 (24 June 1996): 45.

Channel in Europe. These properties make up 25% of NBC's asset base.[49]

In August 1996, Tom Rogers, president of NBC Cable, announced that NBC's long-range plans are to launch MSNBC networks in Europe and Asia. He said that the network will customize Internet versions of MSNBC in a handful of European and Asian countries. "Having some cable programming on all four of our channels in Europe and Asia that is flagged as MSNBC . . . will help develop the Internet awareness for the network."[50]

# ABC

The ABC network, with approval of its parent, Walt Disney Co., announced its intention to start a 24-hour news network in April 1996. By May of the same year, it had folded the cable news effort. The reason given was a startling move by Rupert Murdoch to offer a one-time cash-for-carriage incentive of between $10 and $11 per subscriber to U.S. cable (and direct to home satellite) operators for channel carriage of the new Fox News Channel in up to 30 million homes. Analysts viewed Murdoch's offer as an effort to show the industry that he was willing to spend whatever it took to get Fox News off the ground. ABC executives did not want to get into a bidding war for distribution. Disney and ABC executives concluded that the cost of entry was too high: at least $400 million in losses in the first five years, and possibly no return on investment until the end of the first decade. They were already looking at losses of hundreds of millions of dollars for at least the first five years.[51] Ironically, this wasn't the first time an upstart cable news operation had spoiled ABC's bid to enter the 24-hour news business. Turner created Headline News and eventually purchased the Satellite News Channel from ABC in 1982 to avoid splitting the market with the broadcasting giant.

---

[49] Amy Cortese and Rob Hof, "Network Meets Net," *Business Week* (15 July 1996): 68.

[50] Jim McConville, "MSNBC Blocks Headed Overseas," *Broadcasting & Cable* 126 (5 August 1996): 63.

[51] McClellan and Brown, 44; Wayne Walley and Jon LaFayette, "ABC Cable News Good as Dead," *Broadcast & Cable* 126 (27 May 1996): 1, 23.

## CBS

CBS network, owned by the Westinghouse company, has made some gestures toward getting into the 24-hour cable and satellite news business. In June 1996, the company acquired the Spanish-language news channel TeleNoticias, which is seeking to convert from a basic news channel to a full-service news and information network to include a roster of original magazine, talk, and other programs. The Miami-based service is now available in 22 Latin American and Caribbean countries, the U.S., and Spain. A separate customized U.S. feed has been developed, which contains much material seen in the Latin American feed based on stories of interest to U.S. Hispanic viewers.[52] The new CNN en Español went head-to-head in competition with TeleNoticias when it launched in March 1997.

CBS TeleNoticias combines the strength of CBS News programming and newsgathering experience with Group W Satellite Communications distribution, sales, and marketing experience. This deal is thought to be a first step for CBS in its plans to expand into the cable and satellite markets and to look further afield. Donald Mitzner, president of Group W Satellite Communications, said he sees the acquisition as a long-term commitment to the international news business.[53]

CNN's *international* competitors are likely to have an even greater impact on Turner's news network in the coming years. And in at least one case, a CNN competitor has a much longer tradition of offering broadcast news services to a global market.

## BBC World

The original BBC World Service broadcast in many languages to virtually the whole world via shortwave radio. The role of the program was to promote the "British way and purpose" with

---

[52] Steve McClellan, "Telenoticias on the Grow," *Broadcasting & Cable* 126 (16 September 1996): 39.

[53] Debra Johnson, "Westinghouse/CBS Gets Global Cable Foothold," *Broadcasting & Cable* 126 (1 July 1996): 14.

much the same intent as the Voice of America and other public diplomacy channels, basically an instrument of government policy.[54]

In 1991, the BBC launched World Service Television, a commercially funded news and entertainment channel with no government support. Its market-by-market approach to channel development meant that it often needed to find commercial partners in each region and use the BBC brand name and product to build up local audiences.[55] While CNN concentrated on breaking news, the BBC intended to adopt a more interpretive approach. While CNN was avowedly commerical, the public service orientation of the BBC would be emphasized. At least these were to be the distinctive features according to BBC propotional materials. In planning for a BBC-WT service to North America, Director of Programs for BBC Worldwide Television Hugh Williams said

> The BBC perspective on the world would be different from the 'clearly American' CNN. . . . BBC has always been international from its start in radio. . . . BBC World wants to have an international perspective with context and analysis, but as a professional and modern news channel. We think the great appeal here will be to see how America is seen through other eyes.[56]

In June 1996, John Birt, director-general of the BBC, announced major restructuring in the news divisions which merged the radio and TV staffs into one team; the World Service was combined with the domestic news division in Britain. The strategy was to cut costs by 15 percent, to invest in digital technology as a part of the plan to go for a 24-hour news channel, to produce additional themed subscription channels and provide CD-quality sound.[57]

---

[54] Chris Bulloch, "BBC Goes Commercial on a Global Scale," *Via Satellite* (August 1994): 14.

[55] Robin Knight, "Global TV News Wars," *U.S. News & World Report* 117 (26 December 1994): 70.

[56] Wayne Walley, "BBC World Coming to U.S.," *Electronic Media* (1 January 1995): 33.

[57] Heidi Dawley, "The BBC as We Know it is Signing Off," *Business Week* (12 August 1996): 50.

Part of the reason for the restructuring was the prospect of un-precedented competition at home and the need to mount a sub-stantially more ambitious service abroad. Digital broadcasting services were expected in Britain on Rupert Murdoch's BSkyB satellite service, which would boost the number of TV channels from 30 to 200-plus in 1997. The BBC forecast that audience share for the four traditional channels—BBC 1 , BBC 2, ITV and Chan-nel 4—would fall to 65 percent from 90 percent within 10 years.[58]

Outside Europe, WST began as a part of Hong Kong-based Star TV, which, like BSkyB, was controlled by Rupert Murdoch's News Corp. BBC WST, now called BBC World, was delivered over AsiaSat1's north beam as part of the Star TV program pack-age, a service that was terminated in late 1994 for one or both of two reasons: 1) that the BBC offended Star TV's most important customer, the People's Republic of China, with unflattering news coverage; 2) that Murdoch did not wish to displease the Chinese and had in mind to offer a global news service of his own. BBC World continued to be carried over the AsiaSat south beam which reached much of Southeast Asia, the Indian subcontinent, and the Middle East, but not the Chinese, Korean, and Japanese markets.[59]

The powerful and ocean-spanning PanAmSat PAS-2 Pacific Ocean region satellite is now used by BBC World to reach viewers throughout the Asia Pacific region. A second PanAmSat satellite, the PAS-4 Indian Ocean region satellite, is used for reception in south Asia. In 1996, BBC World improved its global distribution by adding coverage of Latin America on the PAS-3 Atlantic Ocean region satellite, which offers a potential audience of 12 million cable and MMDS households. Its digital video signal is uplinked to the satellite in Ku-band from the U.K. and then broadcast to cable headends on the C-band Pan American beam. Also in 1996, BBC World became part of the Galaxy Latin Amer-ica DirecTv digital package aimed at home viewers in Brazil,

---

58 Ibid.

59 Bulloch, 14.

Mexico, and Venezuela, with the rest of Latin America to be targeted in 1997.[60]

## Fox News

The 24-hour Fox News channel and the Fox News Web site[61] were launched in October 1996 from new headquarters in New York City, the initiative of Rupert Murdoch, whose long-term goal is to be "the first truly global media power with access to nearly two-thirds of the world's population."[62]

> Our plan is very simple: we are expanding a global platform for the distribution of video and information. We are embracing the digital revolution. . . . We will be taking Fox News globally, first in Britain this year on BSkyB, and then the whole of Europe. And certainly in Southwest Asia, India and Australia in the first half of next year through our existing distribution channels there. . . We are trying to establish a global distribution platform because we know how difficult it has been to launch any kind of product on cable in this country.[63]

Fox News' strategy has been to negotiate distribution agreements in the U.S. with the big cable operators until it can launch its own ASkyB direct satellite service (in conjunction with MCI) in 1997. TCI, Comcast, Continental cable and others signed up under the financially attractive cash-per-subscriber package offered by Murdoch, which gave the Fox News Channel access at launch to an estimated 12 million cable subscribers.[64] Fox thought it had an agreement with Time Warner Cable as well, which would have assured it an additional 10 million viewers, the critical mass presumed to be needed to compete with CNN's 70 million and

---

[60] Glen Dickson, "BBC Worldwide Television," *Broadcasting & Cable* 126 (18 November 1996): 80.

[61] See http://www.foxnews.com.

[62] Ronald Grover, "Murdoch vs. Everyone," *Business Week* (9 December 1996): 75.

[63] Mermigas, "The Murdoch Map," *Electronic Media* (7 October 1996): 6.

[64] Price Colman, "TCI Will Carry Fox News Channel," *Broadcasting & Cable* 126 (1 July 1996): 48.

MSNBC's 21 million viewers in the U.S. market. At the last minute, Time Warner chose not to carry the Fox News Channel, deciding to offer its cable availablity to MSNBC instead.[65]

Fox News will depend heavily on its 10 domestic and international bureaus, its own newspapers and television stations, and strategic alliances with Reuters, WTN, and AP for content. The cost, according to Murdoch, will be about $140 million to launch, with an annual budget of about $100 million. Revenues will start at $50 million and then rise.[66] Fox News chief Roger Ailes has said the cable channel will work at combating what some believe is the media's "liberal bias."[67] He stressed that Fox News will offer fair and balanced content. The channel will clearly label commentary and opinion to distinguish them from news.[68] When questioned about the viability of Fox News, Ailes responded,

> They said Fox couldn't be a network, Fox couldn't do sports, Fox can't do news. And every time they turn around, Rupert Murdoch does it because Rupert Murdoch gets things done.[69]

As for his immediate competitors CNN and MSNBC, Ailes was hesitant to predict any shakeout. "There may be room for five or six," he wrote, "we don't know."[70]

As a result of the confrontation in New York, in which fox News was denied carriage on Time Warner cable systems, Murdoch has threatened to take Turner and Time Warner services off

---

[65] Mermigas, "Murdoch Vows Action Against Time Warner," *Electronic Media* (23 September 1996): 1, 30. In September 1996, Time Warner chose MSNBC to fulfill its agreement with the U.S. Federal Trade Commission, which had stipulated that as a condition of its $6.8 billion acquisition of TBS, Time Warner must offer its cable subscibers a second cable news service.

[66] Mermigas, 6.

[67] Lee Hall, "Arch-Conservative to Host Fox Cable Show," *Electronic Media* (26 August 1996): 32.

[68] Jon LaFayette, "Fairness Will Set Fox News Apart," *Electronic Media* (9 September 1996): 3.

[69] McClellan and Brown, 44.

[70] Rich Brown, "Fox Unveils News Channel Lineup," *Broadcasting & Cable* 126 (9 September 1996): 47-48.

News Corp.–controlled program delivery systems in Asia, Australia, and Western Europe. These include the Star TV satellite service operating out of Hong Kong and the BSkyB satellite service headquartered in London.[71] In 1996 News Corp. made arrangements to join a DBS (direct to home satellite) service to Latin America in a joint venture with partners Televisa, PanAmSat, Globo, and TCI.[72] In addition, News Corp. has secured permission from India's Foreign Investment Promotion Board (FIPB) to establish a wholly owned TV company in India. The protectionist government of India has approved an $11 million direct investment in the company, called News Television India Private Ltd.[73]

News Corp. is involved in creating a digital multi-channel satellite platform for Japan, dubbed JSkyB, in cooperation with the Japanese Softbank Corp. Murdoch was in Japan in June 1996 seeking to expand on his current satellite holdings, which include BSkyB in the U.K., ASkyB in the U.S., and Star TV in Asia services. His Star Plus service, which airs a 24-hour Japanese language version of Star TV to an estimated one million homes via cable was begun in April 1996 as an all-digital service. Softbank Corp. and News Corp. agreed to a joint venture, owned equally by both parties, which will acquire 100 percent of the shares of Obunsha Media Co., Ltd. which holds 5,136 shares, or 21.4 percent of shares, of Asahi National Broadcasting Company, Ltd., ironically CNN's most important affiliate.[74]

---

71 Mermigas, 30.

72 Mermigas, 6.

73 Debra Johnson and Nicole McCormick, "News Corp. In India," *Broadcasting & Cable* 126 (16 September 1996): 59.

74 "News Corp. to Launch JSkyB," *Japan Times* (13 June 1996): 14.

IT IS SO INTERESTING TO SEE *how some of us have different perceptions of how to cover news. While people were only too eager to criticize CNN for a U.S. or Euro-centric attitude toward news coverage, I thought: "How much coverage do these same people who live in the metropolis tend to give to their far-flung districts? Let alone free coverage that they would give them without editorializing?" For example in Bharain, how much coverage does the Suni minority let the Shiite majority have? Would they let the Shiites have two hours a week of unfettered airtime on Bahrain TV? It's always an eye-opening experience at each [contributors] conference. It's nice to see the big shots, but for me the more valuable experience is to see my [World Report] colleagues. A fellow from the Middle East, who told me he is the Larry King of the Middle East, was siting next to me and says, "Larry King is great. He is my idol and I love him. But don't you think he is a little bit too Jewish?" I am Jewish. How can I answer him? I look forward to those kinds of gems.*

Stewart Krohn*
General Manager, TV Channel 5, Belize

---

* Interview (August 1996).

# 7

# CNN's International Partners

*They say CNN is not about the building or about Atlanta, because it just goes to show, they can give you news from any part of the world, right? They have a satellite in an attache case and that's it! They can broadcast from all over the world, so it's irrelevant where you are.*[1]

On December 17, 1996, a Tuesday evening, the Japanese ambassador to Peru was hosting a reception at his residence in Lima. Some 500 distinguished guests, mainly from the business and diplomatic community of Lima, were celebrating with their Japanese hosts the birthday of Emperor Hirohito. As the party was in full swing, but soon after the U.S. ambassador had left, the Japanese ambassador's residence was surrounded by an armed group of Peruvian rebels of the Tupac Amaru Revolutionary Movement. All guests were taken hostage.

Yan Mei and Chris Turner were on the International Desk at CNN in Atlanta when news of the hostage situation in Peru broke. Recognizing the story's importance, they called their senior editor Stephen Cassidy at home. Cassidy immediately went to CNN Center to begin wrestling with how best to cover the story. When he began receiving calls from TV Asahi in Japan, he understood that the events transpiring in Lima were significant to CNN not only for their intrinsic news value, but because the story was of great importance to one of the oldest and most valued affiliates of CNN.

---

[1] Karen Davila (reporter, GMA-TV7 Philippines), interview (August 1996).

At about 6 A.M., Cassidy strode over to the satellites and circuits desk, situated on the perimeter of the newsroom, and told Duty Manager Libby Barnett he was thinking of sending one of the CNN fly-aways and a crew to Peru. He needed to know whether CNN could get good pictures out of Peru and, if so, which space segments could be reserved for satellite transmission. Barnett promptly called the Washington office of Intelsat and the Atlanta office of PanAmSat, the two international space communication operators working in the region. With some difficulty, she secured satellite capacity.

Cassidy meanwhile had brought in Eason Jordan, who would need to sign off on the considerable expenditures entailed by the satellite time and the travel, maintenance, and overtime costs of the crew for a stay of indefinite duration. There was no way of knowing whether the hostage crisis would last one day or ten or a hundred. The fact that CNN's Japanese partner TV Asahi had a vital interest in the story was a factor in the decision to commit to a week's lease on an Intelsat transponder.

CNN shortly afterward learned that Pan-Tel TV, a regional consortium of broadcasters, already was covering the story. Pan-Tel had a link via its own dish aimed at the PanAmSat satellite and was able to feed pictures to CNN until the Atlanta-based news organization could get its own crews and equipment into the country. Barnett immediately began the tortuous process of calling and telexing the Peruvian state regulatory and customs agencies. The staff of the CNN Spanish channel helped her deal with those in Peru having approval authority over CNN camera and satellite equipment entering the country and making use of the national airwaves.

It was almost 36 hours before the equipment and crew arrived in Lima. Even though the approvals came relatively quickly, the CNN crew and its 25 cases of equipment were stuck in Houston, unable to fit onto a commercial airliner. Jordan approved the charter of a plane that could accommodate all equipment and the crew. Once in Peru, the crew took less than two hours to set up and transmit the first pictures back to Atlanta. In Atlanta, the news of the hostage crisis was quickly packaged for airing on the various CNN networks, and CNN Newsource prepared video material for distribution to CNN's 380 domestic and 200 international affiliates.

## CNN Affiliates

Two weeks later, with the hostage situation still unresolved, Eason Jordan reflected on recent events:

> This is a huge story for TV Asahi. It is the ambassador's residence and many Japanese officials and citizens are involved. In this unique case, I don't know if there is another [CNN-affiliate relationship] with which it can be compared. We are giving TV Asahi priority access to the dish, even ahead of CNN. TV Asahi, just within the past week, has probably done more than 100 live and taped transmissions via that portable CNN uplink in Lima.[2]

Jordan explained that CNN's relationship with TV Asahi, the largest private and commercial broadcaster in Japan, goes back to 1982, just two years after the launch of the CNN 24-hour news channel in the United States. According to Jordan, although CNN has many strong partners around the world, its relationship with TV Asahi is unique because of the faith that TV Asahi

> showed in us in the early days of CNN when there were not many believers. Because the roots were planted so long ago, and have grown over time to a wide-ranging relationship, it would be fair to say that TV Asahi is our most important and valued affiliate internationally. In the sense that the relationship has many facets to it including the sharing of a bureau in Bangkok, Thailand and sharing of newsgathering facilities on various stories around the world on an ad hoc basis. TV Asahi is the only international affiliate with an office and full-time representation in CNN headquarters here in Atlanta. And TV Asahi is a shareholder in a Japanese cable company called JCTV which distributes CNN programs in Japan. So it is a multi-faceted relationship that is much to the benefit of both organizations.[3]

---

[2] Eason Jordan (senior vice president, CNN), interview (December 1996).

[3] Ibid.

As for TV Asahi's use of the CNN uplink in Peru, Jordan said that

> had we been charging full-rate the cost could have been upwards of a half-million dollars in the last week or so. But TV Asahi is an important affiliate of CNN and will receive substantial discounts. CNN will simply defray its very substantial cost; it will not seek to make a profit.[4]

Barnett noted that another important CNN affiliate, n-TV (Germany), used CNN's uplink in Peru, as did SBS-Seoul, and that discounts are frequently given by management in such cases because they are CNN's partners.

One other reason, perhaps less obvious, why CNN went out of its way to accommodate the Japanese broadcaster in covering its international story-of-the-year in South America is that Rupert Murdoch has bought into the parent company of TV Asahi. In 1996, Softbank Corp. of Japan and Murdoch's News Corp. established a joint venture, owned equally by the two parties, which has acquired the Obunsha Media Co., Ltd., a Japanese media company that holds about 25 percent of the shares of Asahi National Broadcasting Company.[5]

## The CNN Connection

It is clear why CNN would wish to establish relationships with broadcasters around the world. It is perhaps less well-understood how local broadcasters benefit and what their motivations are for joining the CNN family, either contractually as an affiliate, as a *World Report* contributor, or both. Answers to these questions are not straightforward, for there are almost as many reasons as there are CNN affiliates and *World Report* contributors. It should be noted that CNN has about the same number of international affiliates as *World Report* has contributing stations—about 200 in each case. About half of the affiliates are *World Report* contributors, meaning that approximately 100 stations around the world

---

[4] Jordan, interview (January 1997).

[5] "News Corp. to Launch JSkyB," *Japan Times* (13 June 1996): 14.

have two connections with CNN—one with CNNI and one with *World Report*.

The reasons for teaming with CNN certainly include extended coverage, which the well-positioned CNN can provide for the local, national, or regional broadcaster. International affiliated stations, such as TV Asahi, that have established formal contracts, own rights to excerpt material from CNN International broadcasts. They are given special rights to receive CNN's *International Newsource*, a twice-a-day regionally customized video feed of international news, or draw on CNN staffing, equipment, and other resources, as in the case of the crisis in Peru, to extend their coverage across the global field.

Less visible are the stations that have something to say but whose news nobody wants. CNN has demonstrated over the years that it is willing to accept news from out-of-the-mainstream broadcasters, that it is willing to carry that news alongside its own, and make it available for others to use. These are the long-standing *World Report* partners, such as SABC–South Africa, whose voice only CNN would carry during the days of apartheid;[6] state broadcasters such as MTV-Hungary, whose reason for affiliation with CNN is, in part, to reach the international diaspora of ethnic Hungarians with news of home; and non-governmental organizations (NGOs), such as the United Nations and the U.N.'s Relief and Works Agency, which have no direct means of communicating to the general public what they are or do.

Some partner stations, both in the public and private sector, make regular local use of stories collected and broadcast by *World Report*. Like many other contributors, Cubavision-Cuba and CMT-Venezuela contribute to *World Report* in part to portray to the global community what life is like in their countries. But they also learn how other stations handle news stories, thereby building the local news organization while enhancing the professional standards of their respective staffs. There also are instances of the individual entrepreneur with a particular story to promote or a

---

[6] SABC is now a CNN affiliate.

theme to advance, who has convinced her or his station to seek the CNN relationship.

# International Visibility

## SABC, South Africa

The South African Broadcasting Corporation is now a CNN affiliate, rebroadcasting up to twelve hours daily of CNNI programming on two channels. There was a time, however, when such a contract would have been impossible. At the time Ted Turner issued his invitation to the world's broadcasters to join the *World Report* newscast and news exchange, economic sanctions were in place against South Africa. For its national racial policies, the country had few friends. With some disbelief and much enthusiasm for the project, the SABC began making regular contributions on the CNN channel. Hein Ungerer, a producer/correspondent for Channel Africa, the overseas news service of the SABC, was one of those assigned the job of preparing reports. Ungerer recalled that

> Those were the days of strict editorial control emanating from state control of the broadcaster. Channel Africa was fully funded by the South African Department of Foreign Affairs and we were therefore editorially required to follow the official government line rigidly. In some cases even stricter than normal SABC internal broadcasts.
>
> Individual contributions were viewed by senior editorial staff to ensure that they carried "the right message." Although individual producers used to try and see what we could "get away with" under the censors, we succeeded infrequently. We tried to steer clear of the heavy political stories as much as possible, preferring to show conditions on the ground and leaving it up to the viewers to draw their own conclusions but from time to time we were instructed to cover certain stories. If our scripts were not "correct" enough they would be rewritten by senior editorial staff.
>
> We became aware that the CNN *World Report* broadcasts were being closely monitored by the South African Embassy in Washington because on several occasions we were hauled through to Pretoria, the country's seat of gov-

ernment, for "overstepping the line" or not carrying the "right message."[7]

The participation of South Africa in the CNN-initiated international newscast and news exchange did cause problems back at CNN Center, not as a result of staff or even viewer complaints but because other African countries such as Nigeria declared they would not participate if South Africa was a member. Managing this stand-off, and another like it that involved the politically divided country of Cyprus, put the diplomatic skills of executive producer Stuart Loory to the test. When the issue came to the fore at the first contributors conference, Loory sought to explain CNN's position to those gathered:

> It is the philosophy of the CNN *World Report* that we be as inclusive as possible, rather than exclusive. That means we are trying to create a true marketplace of viewpoints and perspectives on the news around the world. We have material from South African Broadcasting Corporation. That is the single, sole, legitimate broadcaster in South Africa. We also take material, as you know, from an organization called South Africa Now/Globalvision, which is headquartered in New York City. South Africa Now/Globalvision meets the kind of criteria that we are talking about. It serves to give the audience of the CNN *World Report* an alternative point of view. Suppose we were to exclude South Africa Now?
>
> I have had some problems, as a matter of fact, with some organizations that have not joined the CNN *World Report* because they do not want to take part in a program that recognizes the SABC as a legitimate, news gathering, news dissemination organization. I have to say to those organizations, "I am sorry, but I cannot be exclusive to accommodate you."[8]

The correspondent from South Africa, in looking back on those days, said that the inclusion of the South African reports in *World Report* impressed him greatly, given the circumstances.

---

[7] Hein Ungerer (producer, Channel Africa/SABC), interview (October 1996).

[8] Quoted in Don Flournoy, *CNN World Report: Ted Turner's International News Coup* (London: John Libbey & Company, 1992): 26.

Contributions actually helped the staff at Channel Africa to do a more critical job. The reporter, Hein Ungerer, remembered that

> an almighty row erupted on the day we first tried to use the words 'universally hated apartheid system'. It did not escape the censor's attention but having been exposed to the South Africa Now contributions gave us a solidarity with a fellow group of South Africans based in New York.

The authors, who attended the first *World Report* Contributors Conference in 1989, reminded Ungerer of the evening that conference participants were taken to visit the Martin Luther King Jr. Memorial in Atlanta. The South African reporter was observed standing alone for much of the outing. Ungerer remembered the evening, and the conference as a whole, all too well.

> I wish more people had spoken to me at the 1989 conference. It was probably one of the most difficult things I ever did, representing the SABC. At that conference the climate was still very hostile, although I must add immediately that from the organizer's side the welcome was warm. I was treated like everyone else. I was probably also oversensitive as I was quite uncomfortable being associated with the SABC but happy to be among broadcasters. It was a great revelation to me, meeting fellow broadcasters from all over the world, and it was exciting to be part of the then-brand-new idea of airing contributions with local flavour intact![9]

One year later, at the 1990 *World Report* conference, Ungerer was put on the program and invited to talk about the changes in South Africa and the future of SABC.

> This happened just after the unbannings. . . . The SABC was very much the flavour of the month at this conference and my acceptance was greatly due to the whole apartheid era's end having been announced. . . . Few of us at that stage thought of the great difficulty still facing us to transform the repressiveness of the white rule era to the rainbow nation democracy we were aiming at.
>
> I moved out of the external services onto mainline South African television shortly after the 1990 Contributors Conference. I joined one of the new "progressive" current

---

[9] Ungerer, interview (October 1996).

affairs shows called *Agenda*. . . . This was an exciting time in the SABC as we were slaughtering holy cows all over the place. The program had live debates on abortion, communism vs. capitalism, censorship—themes the SABC had never handled before, least of all *live*.

When I spoke at the 1990 Contributors Conference, I pointed out that the broadcasting of CNN overall in South Africa started a television news revolution by South Africans for the first time being allowed to see *live* and *uncensored* broadcasting. It set a new standard for television journalists and was the beginning of the end for state control. With the unbanning of the liberation movements in the same year the wheel started turning in all earnest and by 1993 we had trainers from the Canadian and Australian Broadcasting Corporations teaching SABC journalists.[10]

SABC continues to contribute to *World Report*, but now it is the television magazine producers and not the news reporters who carry out the task. "The stories we send to CNN *World Report* are a shortened version of the magazine inserts," according to Christa Cameron and Anne Hutchison, the current contributors. Their greatest difficulty is finding the time to re-edit these pieces for *World Report*, as this is a voluntary exercise that cannot interfere with their assigned duties in producing stories for Good Morning South Africa. According to Hutchison,

Since the transformation initiated with elections in 1994, there has been a huge interest in South Africa and its peoples, especially since the changeover was peaceful. I think our programs can reflect the harmonizing and integration that is taking place. . . . The freeing of the country has meant a freeing of the airwaves. Whereas before everything was quite literally in black and white and that was the way the world perceived our country. We are now able to report on absolutely anything that we think is of interest to a viewer, whether that be in South Africa or in the rest of the world, which is what democracies are all about.[11]

---

10 Ibid.

11 Anne Hutchison (producer, SABC), interview (October 1996).

Both Cameron and Hutchison have participated in CNN's International Professional Program (IPP), Cameron in June 1995 and Hutchison in January 1996.

Ironically, the change in South Africa's political system has meant that the satellite services that formerly were used to get SABC's up-to-the-minute stories to Atlanta and the *World Report* staff—which had eagerly anticipated the arrival of such timely material for the daily and weekend shows—no longer are available. Instead, material must be sent by courier service twice a week, necessitating the contribution of less "time-bound" material, according to Hutchison.

Tseliso Leballo, newly appointed head of SABC's news bureaus in nine South African provinces including Free State and Northern Cape, was in Atlanta in December 1996. His goal was to negotiate with CNN a custom-made IPP-type training program for 24 newspeople, to be selected from the various bureaus. According to Tseliso,

> We need to be studying the way things are done at CNN. From mid-next year SABC will have competitors. IBA [Independent Broadcast Authority] has begun deregulation, starting with the country's radio stations. SABC is preparing for competitors.[12]

## Cubavision, Cuba

Two countries representative of those most often left out of world news are Cuba and Angola. It is noteworthy that each of these countries, one Latin American and the other African, were on the wrong side of the Cold War to earn much coverage—other than the stereotypical Soviet-puppet treatment—from the western press. To counteract such reporting, Cubavision became a contributor to *World Report* when it began in 1987, and since 1989 has aired its own version of *World Report* in Cuba. In prime time, hundreds of contributed pieces from around the world have

---

[12] Tseliso Leballo (regional head of news bureaus, SABC), interview (December 1996).

appeared on a dubbed 30-minute version of Sunday's CNN *World Report* in Havana.

Armando Jimenes, news director of Cubavision Internacional, noted with appreciation that *World Report* offers broadcasters such as Cubavision the means—albeit fraught with difficulty—to present to television viewers around the world stories from their unique perspective.

> Present-day journalism makes people, places, events, and even wars fashionable. But, what happens when they are no longer news? We end up being as empty and ignorant as we were before. CNN *World Report* offers a unique opportunity to prevent this from happening. In contributing to *World Report* we seek to show the country the way the people see it, providing an extensive coverage that ranges from crises to daily happenings.
>
> Sometimes it's hard for us to maintain a coherent news policy [regarding our contributions to *World Report*]. Even though we are one of the closest CNN contributors, geographically speaking, we cannot send our reports regularly due to the poor relations between Cuba and the United States. Therefore, immediacy is out of the question and we have to report on "timeless" stories.[13]

Jimenes also noted the difficulty experienced in receiving feedback on submitted reports.

> On just a few occasions, we've had direct accounts of our contributions, especially when we report on scientific and technical subjects. For instance, some viewers have contacted us in order to obtain additional information on anti-drug treatment in Cuba or the cure of retinitis pigmentosa (an eye disease). We know that in the past CNN received letters referring to Cuba's contributions. An exerpt from one of those letters was published once in the mailbox section.[14]

The Sunday *World Report* program that airs on Cuba-vision is popular among viewers and Cuban media scholars. According to

---

[13] Armando Jimenes (news director, Cubavision), interview (October 1996).

[14] Stuart Loory, the founder of the program, for a time included a segment in the program when he read some of the viewer responses to contributed stories.

Jimenes, the *World Report* "standard out" — what reporters say at the end of their package to sign off —

> has even become a popular phrase that you can often hear in the streets. . . . *World Report* has also aroused a lot of interest as a communications phenomenon. Journalism students at the Communications School of the University of Havana have written two theses on the show.[15]

Ted Turner has said that it was Cuban President Fidel Castro who inspired him to make CNN an international service:

> When I started CNN, I really didn't have any intention to go outside the United States with the service. In fact, where I got the idea that the service was of value in other countries was from Fidel Castro in Cuba. When our film crews were in Cuba [in 1982], we were told by a member of Cuban television that President Castro would like to meet me, if there is an opportunity to do so. I accepted the invitation and went and spent a week in Cuba, seeing Cuban television and the various ministries and it was my first opportunity to visit a socialist country. I had all the same prejudices and preconceived notions that most people in the capitalist world had ten years ago, that when I went down there, I was going into where the enemy was, I might be kidnapped, never come home, and so forth and so on.
>
> In fact, the stereotypes that had been presented to me in the media were . . . When I got to Havana, I thought I would see everybody walking around with their ball in their hand that was chained to their leg, with tanks on every corner and machine guns and a very unhappy group of people. And in fact, people were wearing different coloured outfits, there were no more police around than there are here in the United States and I had great conversations. . . . But the whole idea is Fidel Castro was watching CNN. He had a satellite dish and he was watching it and he said it was very important for him to find out what was going on in the world.[16]

---

15 Jimenes, interview (October 1996). Mayra Rego Franco, "CNN *World Report*," masters thesis (1990), and Roberto Cospedes and Lissette Gomez, "The News on CNN *World Report*," masters thesis (1993).

16 Quoted in Flournoy, 6–7.

In August 1996, CNN received permission from Castro to become the first American-based news organization in almost 30 years to set up a full-time newsgathering operation in Havana. Regulations stemming from Washington's economic embargo against Cuba required CNN to obtain a license from the Treasury Department to establish a permanent bureau there, permission that it received in February 1997 following an endorsement from Senator Jesse Helms.[17] Earlier, Gil Kapen, staff director of the U.S. House subcommittee on the Western Hemisphere, had told a forum on "The Future of Free Press in Cuba" that he favored the opening of U.S. news bureaus in Cuba, and predicted it will happen "once the kinks are worked out." But approval came slowly, in part, explained Kapen, because lawmakers have worried that American journalists

> have traded their integrity as journalists for access to Cuba. In the past, U.S. journalists have pulled their punches, failing to present an honest image of Castro's human rights abuses in exchange for permission to work temporarily on the island.[18]

CNN President Tom Johnson balked at such a characterization:

> CNN is a tool of information. It really does not attempt to press any agenda on the world. We are not anti-Castro or pro-Castro. We are not anti–PRC or pro–PRC, not anti–Saddam Hussein or pro-Saddam Hussein. We are trying to inform the world about the issues of the world—population issues, environmental issues, health issues, government issues, culture issues, surely issues that relate to war and peace—but [CNN's principal mission] is to reveal to this planet the news of the planet.[19]

Johnson also has argued that the U.S. State Department should be more flexible in making it possible for *World Report*

---

[17] Larry Rohter, "In Trying to Get Into Cuba, CNN Hits Snags at Home," *New York Times* (13 January 1997): D1.

[18] "The Future of the Free Press in Cuba," Columbia University Media Studies Center, Freedom Forum (20 December 1996). See: http://www.   mediastudies.org.

[19] Tom Johnson (president, CNN), interview with Paolo Ghilardi (December 1996).

contributors from Cuba to attend the contributors conferences in Atlanta. He noted the difficulties CNN has had in arranging visas for contributors from Cuba, Iraq, Libya, and Vietnam.

> I think it is unfortunate that they continue to deny visas to a conference such as this. If there is anything that would seem to serve the cause of a better world it is communications.[20]

He described with some pride the occasion during the May 1994 *World Report* Contributors Conference when a Cuban reporter asked a question of President Bill Clinton during the *Global Forum*.

> This was the first time since before the [Cuban] revolution that a Cuban reporter has been able to ask a question of the president of the United States. It happened here.[21]

## TPA-Angola

Angola was, until the late 19th century, a major embarcation port for the slave trade on the west coast of Africa, and until 1975 a colonial holding of the Portuguese. When it gained independence, Angola almost immediately was trapped in a regional conflict that was an outgrowth of the Cold War. Having aligned itself with the Soviet Union, Angola found itself the target of western powers, led by the United States, who expended enormous financial and military capital to support a rebel leader who controlled much of the interior of the country. For 17 years, the Cold War was waged as a hot, brutal battle on the bloodfields of Angola. With the fall of the Soviet Union in 1991, the United States began the process of officially recognizing the government of Jose Eduardo dos Santos — in effect changing sides in the conflict — bringing into the newly-democratized government Joseph Savimbi, whose U.S.- and South African-backed forces had done so much to destroy the country and its economy.

Leif Biureborgh, a longtime Swedish consultant to the state broadcaster, TPA-Angola, brought Angola into the CNN family

---

[20] Johnson, interview with authors (December 1996).

[21] Ibid.

by helping it make contributions to the *World Report* program beginning in 1988. Biureborgh remembered that

> At that time Angola was still a one-party state. In December 1988 the Angolan government signed the New York accords together with Cuba and South Africa. These accords gave independence to Namibia and started the withdrawal of the Cuban troops in Angola. The international atmosphere was then strongly influenced by perestroika in the Soviet Union which also was reflected on the societal climate in Angola.
>
> The contacts with the *World Report* came at the right moment, and could then inspire and give impetus to a new and open style of journalism, thus abandoning the old *Pravda* style which hitherto had prevailed. I am fortunate to have assisted in this very important change. The *World Report* linkage contributed immensely, and also even legalized the general sweeping use of parabolic antennas which definitely opened the country for the international media. In the first row was CNN, introduced via CNN *World Report*.[22]

Biureborgh noted that the TPA contributions to *World Report* have increased through the years in quantity as well as improving in quality, so that by the end of 1994 there was a contribution nearly every week.

> These contributions had to compensate for the lack of interest shown by international media for the Angolan civil war whose tragic dimensions have been too frequently overshadowed by the conflicts in Bosnia and in the Middle East. All this despite the fact that the United Nation's largest peace operation in the world is since 1994 being carried out in Angola.[23]

As one who has frequently attended the *World Report* conferences in Atlanta, often with the minister of information and the director of TPA-Angola, he said he is

> convinced that the frequency and quality of the TPA contributions have had some impact on the awareness of the existence of Angola among the CNN/CNNI/TBS personnel and their global audience. It is also very positive that such

---

[22] Leif Biureborgh (consultant, TPA-Angola), interview (July 1996).

[23] Ibid.

> excellent personal relationships have been developed with a variety of persons on all levels in the whole of the CNN organization.[24]

He said he is convinced that viewers in the United States and in Europe are warming up to the *World Report*,

> and that the TPA contributions are being observed and appreciated. . . . The reason for the popularity of the *World Report* is that it represents diversity and variety in views and perspective in comparison to the big news agencies who all try to look the same all over the world. It is clear that the media niche that the *World Report* represents is both unique and authentic and consequently attracts a growing global audience.[25]

What is remarkable about the Angolan contributions is that they have been achieved despite the ongoing problems facing the TPA-Angola staff in Luanda.

> Angola is a country with weak infrastructures. Consequently transports, communications, logistics systems and a chaotic economy combined with the uncertainty of a yet not resolved civil conflict are daily obstacles. An important difficulty is the lack of qualified personnel in translating from English to Portuguese; vice versa is still more difficult.[26]

## Cyprus (North and South)

Neither Bayrak-TV, North Cyprus, nor CYBC-TV Greek Cyprus is a contractual affiliate of CNN. Yet, almost every week for ten years, they have each contributed stories from their perspective to CNN *World Report*. 1996 was an eventful year for the two stations, as tensions escalated sharply on the politically divided island and, more often than not, they were the only ones there to report the news.

The history of the Cyprus conflict is an old one based on cultural and language differences between the island's ethnic Greek

---

[24] Ibid.

[25] Ibid.

[26] Ibid.

population and its Turkish minority. In 1974, the island became divided when Turkey invaded and proclaimed a independent republic in the north, an act which was condemned by the U.N. Security Council. As of 1997, U.N. peacekeepers remain stationed on the "green belt" dividing north and south.

The issue of who would be eligible to represent Cyprus in *World Report* was publically, and heatedly, aired in 1989 at the first *World Report* Contributors Conference in Atlanta. Themis Themistocleous, the contributor from CYBC-TV, declared to Executive Producer Stuart Loory and those gathered at the conference that

> There is no Turkish Cyprus, as there is no Greek Cyprus. There is no North, as there is no South. No Arctic Cyprus, as there is no Antarctic Cyprus. There is one state, one country, the Republic of Cyprus, part of which is under foreign occupation. This position is confirmed by the United Nations, the Non-Aligned movement, the Commonwealth, the European Community, the Council of Europe and the community of nations with the exception of one country, Turkey, which is the occupation power. [We appreciate that CNN] is free to invite anyone. We only want to point out that CNN is, regrettably we believe, being taken advantage of in this case by an illegal regime to promote itself via its station.[27]

Loory responded by arguing that CNN was not in the business of recognizing or not recognizing political jurisdictions. In the case of Cyprus, he said, CNN acknowledged that the Turkish Republic of Northern Cyprus is recognized only by one other country in the world and that is Turkey.

> We also understand that Bayrak Television is an organization that meets two criteria that we have for inclusion in the CNN *World Report*. One is that it has a group of people who are known as professional journalists, who are preparing news reports and in some way disseminating those reports. The other criteria is that it has some way of taking the CNN *World Report* [for further use and dissemination]. . . Yours is not the only situation in which we have problems. And I ask you, as you make your protest and as we recognize that protest, to also recognize that there are many other

---

[27] Quoted in Flournoy, 25.

situations around the world where something like this can come up.[28]

Henry Schuster, a *World Report* producer at the time, recently recalled that Loory and staff struggled long over how to handle the deep and historic political differences of opinion among contributing stations. "We were clear this was not about governments, this was about broadcasters," Schuster said;

> For a time we were getting dueling pieces from the Turks and the Bulgarians, about the whole issue of ethnic Turks living in Bulgaria, about how they were treated. One of the legacies of the Ottoman Empire was that there were a lot of Turks living in Bulgaria. It had been the practice of the Bulgarian government to try to wipe away their Turkish heritage by making them change their names, by not letting them identify with things Turkish. These sorts of ethnic conflicts we were getting a taste of before the Cold War was over.
>
> [In their reports] Bulgarian TV was placing great emphasis on how the Turkish minorities were not interested in their Turkish heritage and that they were well-integrated into the mainstream of Bulgarian life. And how there were provocations from the Turkish government. Whereas, you would get pieces in the same timeframe from Turkish TV taking the side of the ethnic minority and reporting on the exodus from Bulgaria into Turkey.[29]

Schuster said the most famous of those exiting Bulgaria was the Olympic weightlifter who reportedly was paid something approaching US$1 million to go over to Turkey.

> We were seeing this drama played out, two governments, two sides, and by the clash of their reports began to get some insight as to what was driving the conflict between them. . . . Through the eyes of Bulgarian TV you would

---

[28] Ibid., 26.

[29] Henry Schuster (senior executive producer, CNN), interview (August 1996). In his opening comments at the 1989 Contributors Conference, Ted Turner only half jokingly said that fighting among contributors must be suspended for the conference in favor of talking. Later, he proclaimed that "We've finally got 'em talkin' to each other instead of fightin'." Quoted in Hank Whittemore, *CNN: The Inside Story* (Boston: Little, Brown and Co., 1990): 276.

have seen that there were some disgruntled people who were not being good Bulgarians and who were being provoked externally. From the eyes of Turkish TV you saw the persecution of the Turkish minority.

In a larger sense, you were seeing a nationalist trend that has now reached full blossom. We are seeing it in the Soviet Union, a reaction to the suppression of nationalist feelings. We were seeing this happen beforehand quite vividly on *World Report*. One week we would get a piece from the Czechs out of Prague and another week we would get a piece out of Bratislava. [30]

Schuster said the *World Report* staff always thought the audience benefited from hearing these different points of view; the benefits gained by CNN were obvious as well, in that

By airing all these events worldwide it helped to enhance CNN's credibility because we had the confidence to air them. . . . Did it enflame things? I don't know. The Greek and Turkish Cypriots were already in conflict. In some sense, it may have also raised people's sensitivities to it, therefore allowing it to be resolved. [31]

In the case of Cyprus, as in numerous other cases involving more than one side to an issue, *World Report* staffers began taking a proactive role in helping each side—whatever its point of view—to make the best case possible. Octavia Nasr, longtime *World Report* assignment editor and co-anchor, remembered that

We were getting great stories from CYBC–Greek Cyprus. Crisp video, excellent English, great natural sound. We were getting bad video from Bayrak-TV, English that was okay, but not as strong as the CYBC packages. [The Turkish side] had opinions but they did not know how to express them, to compete with what we were getting from CYBC. Because of the intimidation, they wouldn't send us stories. I kept calling them, kept sending them faxes. I didn't want them to drop [out]. I got a lot of help from their representative in Washington and he would communicate back to Cyprus.

---

[30] Ibid.

[31] Ibid.

> One of my recommendations to Bayrak-TV was to get someone who is as fluent [in English] as Vivienne [Lymbouris-Loizides]. She is Greek Cypriot. She works for the government station on the Greek side. She is going to give that point of view. She is very articulate, very clear, very straightforward. If you want to compete with her, get someone of that caliber [to represent your point of view]. This is exactly what happened between the two, between Ece Umar and Vivienne Lymbouris-Loizides, they were equal.[32]

Octavia had recently scheduled live interviews for the *World Report* program in which both sides appeared. It was the week of October 7, 1996, when there were violent clashes at the border in which several persons were killed. In her role as anchor,

> I started the interview with the reporter from Northern Cyprus telling us their side of the story. Then we let it all out for the two to tell us this side and that. The whole world is condemning the Turkish Cypriots for killing the Greek Cypriots, but no one is talking about how it all happened. There was a provocation. Now does that mean you shoot someone in the head or beat them to death?, which was my question. Does this explain the killing? Why not arrest them? Then the [Northern Cyprus] reporter is telling us that warnings were given. The guy climbing the flag pole was told he would be shot.

> The next morning IBA-TV [in Israel] picked up the entire segment and aired it in their *Good Morning Israel* show translated into Hebrew. That was one piece of TV that was relevant not only for *World Report* contributors but to an entire region. On the same show they heard both sides of the story.

> When you have a story like this you always have one party that calls and says thank you. In this case it wasn't the Greek Cypriot station that called. It was the Turkish side. And someone here at CNN who is Turkish also sent me an e-mail thanking me for doing this.[33]

---

[32] Octavia Nasr (assignment editor, *World Report*), interview (December 1996).

[33] Ibid.

## UNTV, New York

The United Nations is not a broadcaster, but its television unit is one of the most prolific contributors to the CNN *World Report*, having sent more than 500 reports in ten years. Its staff includes a team of correspondents who travel around the world shooting video and gathering information on various U.N. projects.

Representatives from UNTV have attended *World Report* contributors conferences from the beginning, and have participated in IPP training sessions. UNTV contributions that have aired on *World Report* have won Contributor Awards, handed out at each conference. *World Report*'s Nasr said UNTV is "one of our best contributors," in part because it goes to places where there are no regular contributors.

> They can get stories from places where we don't get stories. For example, this Sunday they are sending us a piece on Sudanese refugees in Uganda. We don't have a Sudanese contributor right now. We don't have a Ugandan contributor. We had them but we lost them. The stories about land mines, about Sri Lanka, Kashmir, the places they get into and the stories they cover are totally different and we need them on *World Report*.[34]

The UNTV's staff members were among the early supporters of the *World Report* idea, as was the United Nations itself. According to a press account from July 1987 — about four months before the launch of the program — CNN planned to have *World Report* anchored from the U.N.[35] But the staff never anticipated including the U.N. or similar organizations as contributors, according to Nasr. Loory and his staff sought out conventional broadcasters, but in the end they accepted "just about anyone who was willing to contribute a piece," Nasr said.

> They ended up with some organizations like UNTV from New York, AMRC [Afghan Media Resource Center] in Pakistan, OECD [Organization for Economic Community

---

[34] Ibid.

[35] Gail Shister, "CBS News Solidly in Third Place," *The Record* (2 July 1987): E13.

Development], and not-for-profit organizations that had an audio-visual section and wanted to contribute.[36]

Eventually, with the growth in the number of *World Report* contributors, the "broadcaster only" policy was enacted, which allowed existing NGO contributors to continue participating but barred new ones, the exceptions being the addition of other U.N. agencies, including UNESCO, which was "a Ted Turner thing," according to Nasr.

> Later on, UNRWA[37] became a separate contributor. Actually, that was a deal made with the Israelis, because they had a problem with PLO-TV being on the show. . . . [So now we] take UNRWA as the voice of the Palestinians under the wing of the U.N.[38]

In the same way that CNN has remained loyal to international broadcasting partners like TV Asahi, *World Report* has been loyal to UNTV, and UNTV in turn has been loyal to *World Report*, according to Nasr.

> They stayed with us. They never miss a show. They are helpful, give us a lot of support. Like last year when we did the U.N. anniversary, we did it up in New York. They helped with everything, the facilities, guidance, information, research. When we did the thing with Boutros Boutros-Ghali—two consecutive years on the *World Report* conference. This year they provided us with four separate reports on U.N. activities around the world to support our coverage. They are a very important part of *World Report*.[39]

## RNTV, Netherlands

Several *World Report* contributing stations, including SwissTV-SRI and Radio TV Netherlands, are public diplomacy broadcasters. Such stations have been established to convey to viewers (and

---

[36] Ibid.

[37] The United Nations Relief and Works Agency, headquartered in Vienna, Austria.

[38] Nasr, interview (December 1996).

[39] Ibid.

listeners) abroad the news of Switzerland and Holland. These organizations, using visual media, function much in the way that radio services such as the Voice of America and BBC World Radio Service have operated for decades. The advantage that being connected to CNN bring, especially the connection with CNN *World Report*, is that their reports have an automatic global audience.

RNTV has been contributing stories to the CNN *World Report* almost from the beginning. The RNTV *World Report* production unit has a budget and three reporters are assigned specifically to produce material for the program. When one of them covers a story, it is produced exclusively for airing on *World Report*. Each week, the three reporters come up with story ideas, which then are scripted, produced, and sent off to Atlanta on a consistent schedule.

Linda van Dort is one of RNTV's contributors to CNN *World Report*. "What Radio Netherlands is about is to present the Netherlands to the rest of the world," she said. "That's in our mandate. . . . 99 percent of it is never broadcasted in the Netherlands." The topics often are the same topics covered by the local stations,

> but the way we go about a story is different, because we know that these stories will be received in other countries, such as in Saudi Arabia. Of course the background of what the Netherlands is about and what the prime minister is about, or whatever, we know is not commonly known in the world, so we take that into consideration.[40]

"The beauty of this program," she said of the *World Report*, is that the reports are not re-edited by CNN before airing.

> We bring stories that we know we would never be able to air, let's say in Saudi Arabia, because it's a particular female subject, or drugs, or whatever. . . . It might be shocking or offensive to other countries, while it is not in the Netherlands. We realize this. Sometimes we don't state things as shockingly as we would be able, in our own country. If it's too shocking, we won't get our message across.
>
> The Netherlands is a country where you can openly discuss issues like drugs and prostitution. You can get a

---

[40] Linda van Dort (RNTV), interview (August 1996).

> prostitute on the screen and a drug shooter on screen. It's a very open society. . . . I did a report on gay marriages, where two men kissed when they got marrried, you know, homosexuals, and everybody was like: "What? Unbelievable!"[41]

But van Dort also noted there are certain types of stories that she will not report.

> CNN asked us to do a story on euthanasia. A man was in the news, a reporter all his life, and he was going to die of cancer. He knew the end was coming and wanted to shorten it, so he taped it all, his death, everything. There was quite a turmoil in Europe. After many discussions we decided not to [send in a story to *World Report*], because about all we could broadcast in two and a half minutes was the actual shot. There would not be enough time to put it into context. If I can't bring it into a good perspective that I can live with, I had rather not touch it.[42]

## MTV-Hungary

Hungarian state television has, as part of its mission, to maintain communication with Hungarians outside the country. Robert Kotroczo, a correspondent for Hungarian television who has attended an IPP training session at CNN, is one of those preparing Hungarian news bulletins for viewers in the United States, news aired weekly on cable channels in places with large Hungarian communities. Cleveland and some parts of California are examples. *World Report* is one of the outlets for news about Hungary prepared by his station.

> My colleagues say that we are just doing propaganda for the government. Which, in a way, is true and not true at the same time. My story on the gulag communism looked pretty good. So I didn't feel bad about that. But, am I going to ask tough questions of the prime minister? I said, "See, we are looking for news, we are interested in NATO, we are

---

[41] Ibid.

[42] Ibid.

interested in the European Union and all that." I am not going to ask him about his new house in the mountains, because I am not interested and probably the world's audience would not be interested either. . . . We do think about the country's image.[43]

## TV Channel 5, Belize

Stewart Krohn is the news director and manager of a broadcast outlet in Belize. His station is not a CNN client but he airs the full two-hour Sunday *World Report* show live. Although he was a reluctant participant in the beginning, he is now pleased with the CNN relationship.

> At the same time that we started contributing to the show, we also started airing the show. Previously, one of our competitors was airing it, but the show never generated much excitement. When we started airing it, our stuff would regularly appear.
>
> The audience really liked the idea of our stuff appearing on one of the world's top news networks. And while it didn't really faze us, because we knew what a mess the show was; to the uninitiated viewer, if you were on CNN, you were on CNN. Whether it was . . . *Larry King Live* or *World Report*, it's CNN.
>
> It really did increase our standing locally. That put us right up there in the big leagues. It's funny. Basically, all those stories that ran on CNN were stories that we had run on our own news. A nice piece that we would run on our own evening newscast, two weeks later shows up on CNN *World Report*. While no one that I know would comment on the newscast, the day after that piece ran on CNN *World Report*, I would run into three people who would tell me: Hey, I saw that story on *World Report*. It was really a good story.
>
> I have to laugh. If you like the two-and-a-half-minute version, you would have really liked the six-minute version that we showed two weeks ago and you never told me anything about. It says something about human nature, I think. You may see your next-door neighbor every day and

---

43 Robert Kotroczo (MTV-Hungary), interview (August 1996).

> never think how good-looking she is, but when you see her
> on TV on the arm of Sylvester Stallone, suddenly she looks
> great.
>
> Whatever it is, by being on the show it tends to make
> us a member of a fraternity of world broadcasters that
> commands a certain amount of respect. If Ted Turner thinks
> my work is good enough to show to the world, it certainly
> commands respect in Belize. It had that hidden bonus for
> us.
>
> While we initially decided to participate because
> somebody asked us nicely, we have since come to see sev-
> eral advantages to it. A second advantage is that, as a pri-
> vate non-governmental broadcaster affected by the vagaries
> of politics in a small country, having or seeming to have
> high-powered friends abroad, makes those in power, who
> might want to make life exceedingly difficult for you, think
> twice before they do what they are inclined to do. That is
> not a benefit that we can quantify, but it is there.[44]

Krohn, like other *World Report* contributors, has wondered at
times why a commercial broadcaster like CNN has attempted to
reverse the flow of news in the world by building a news exchange which lets everybody participate;

> I have no idea why Ted Turner did that. It has certainly
> made him a world of friends. If something earth-shattering
> ever did happen here, just because of the relationship, CNN
> would be the first one I would call. Certainly not NBC,
> ABC, or CBS, though I have worked with those esteemed
> networks many times. CNN just asks nicely.[45]

## Artear Channel 13, Argentina

Argentina's Channel 13 is an important client of CNN. The station has sent at least two employees to the IPP training program,
including senior reporter Juan Micelli. In Micelli's view, that any
station in the world can gain prestige by working with CNN, and

---

[44] Stewart Krohn (general manager and news director, TV Channel 5, Belize),
interview (August 1996).

[45] Ibid.

in turn the stations give prestige to CNN. There is great mutual benefit in being part of an international network that gathers reporters from all over the world on a single show.

> For me personally, in my career it is prestigious to have on my resume that I collaborate with CNN *World Report*. It also gives me a chance to improve my professional talent. Recently, I joined the Turner family as a member of the IPP. It was very positive to be at CNN and exchange experiences with them about how [the news business] works. I appreciated very much the structure and the resources they have. On this side of the world we are more used to improvise than they are at CNN. They are too organized from my point of view. You know, we Latins like to be at the edge every once in a while.

> What I am trying to do is to combine these two aspects. To be more organized. And also have some passion in the job. These two aspects combined makes a good combination. . . . It was a hard time. When I came back, many people told me: what do you think this is, CNN? This is Argentina. We are Latins and Channel 13. Slowly I am trying to change little things that might improve our news department.

> I would say it's prestigious to work with CNN. It is a big opportunity to learn. After all, television was invented by the United States. It was very good for me to see how it works.[46]

## TV Globo, Brazil

TV Globo of Brazil is the fourth-largest commercial TV network in the world and an important client of CNN. In the early 1990s, largely because Paulo Henrique Amorim, the network's New York bureau chief at the time, talked TV Globo executives into it, the South American broadcaster began contributing to *World Report*. Since that time it has won Contributor Awards for Best Feature story, and has sent at least four staff people to the IPP

---

[46] Juan Micelli (senior reporter, Artear Channel 13, Argentina), interview (August 1996).

training program. The participation of Globo did not go unnoticed in the Brazilian media, according to Amorim.

> [I have been invited] a couple of times to be interviewed by CNN when there were big things going on in Brazil like elections or the corrections crisis. I remember that an important Brazilian paper made a story on how TV Globo was now trying to convey their perception of Brazilian problems worldwide [through *World Report*]. This gives you some idea of the impact of CNN on Brazilian viewers.[47]

Amorim said contributing to *World Report* also has given him visibility in the United States, which has opened doors for him when covering stories there. He often has called upon the *World Report* office in Atlanta for video and *World Report* has frequently helped him gain access to editing space during his travels within and outside the United States. The most significant advantage of his *World Report* affiliation was none of these, however, according to Amorim;

> You know cable is something very new in my country, but it reaches the elite crowd in Brazil, the cream of the crop, the ones who call the shots. The minute I got on the air with *World Report*, the way this elite perceived me and my work, the way TV Globo's work in New York City was perceived, changed for the better. It helped Globo tell the Brazilian audience that we were ready to participate in a joint effort like *World Report* on a [professional] basis, doing good stories with good text and pictures. According to international standards, they saw that we could do a good job. So the first impact was in Brazil, how TV Globo and I myself were perceived in Brazil.[48]

Amorim told about a time he was covering a story in Cuba. The *World Report* assignment editor in Atlanta, Debra Daugherty, had helped him with contacts at Cubavision, from whom he got technical help with editing and feeding the TV Globo satellite signal.

---

[47] Paulo Henrique Amorim (former New York bureau chief, TV Globo, Brazil), interview (August 1996).

[48] Ibid.

> I was in Cohema, a beach outside of Havana, at the peak of the [Cuban refugee exodus], where the Cubans were trying to reach the south of Florida by any kind of boat they could get. When we arrived at this beach—which incidentally is the place were the main character of Hemingway's *Old Man and the Sea* lived—there were a bunch of TV crews already there. I remember that one of the [Cuban] guys who was putting together a boat, he looked around and said, "I will talk to all of you. But first I will talk to this guy from CNN." I said, "I am with Globo." He said, "No, no, I saw you on CNN."[49]

He told of a similar incident in Mexico. He was covering the story of a Chinese boat that was on its way to the United States. The U.S. Coast Guard prevented it from entering U.S. territorial waters. The boat had gone to Mexico and had stopped in Ensenata. One of the Mexican public officials approached him and said, "I will talk to you in private because you are from CNN." Amorim told him, "No, no, the guy from CNN is over there." He said, "I know you are from Globo but you are from CNN as well. So I will talk to you."[50]

> Also, in Africa, when there was an outbreak of cholera during the refugee crisis in Rwanda. The fact that I was a *World Report* contributor helped me get an interview with the organization, Doctors Without Borders, operating in one of the refugee camps in Zaire. A woman doctor from Holland working there recognized me because she had seen me on CNN *World Report* when she was stationed in Angola. She could speak some Portuguese so we used Portuguese as a way of communicating.[51]

Daugherty noted that Amorim conducted one of the early interviews with Sub-comandante Marcos, the guerrilla leader in Chiapas, Mexico, who had given his first interview with the Mexican station, Televisa. The second to get access to him was ABC News, and Globo was third, ahead of CNN. The *World*

---

[49] Ibid.

[50] Ibid.

[51] Ibid.

*Report* staff pitched Amorim's video to CNN Spanish and CNN used some of it as well.

But TV Globo's foreign news editor, Simone Duarte, noted that the impact of her station's relationship with CNN goes beyond the acquisition of any single, specific story; rather,

> It's a unique way [for CNN] to have a different perspective, an international perspective. When I was at CNN I talked with Tom Johnson and I said to him, "It's not enough to have different faces in your program, like one anchor is Chinses, the other anchor is Lebanese, the other anchor is from Pakistan. If you don't have people *thinking* international, if everybody is American or everybody is Chinese, you have to have other people that have responsibility to put things on the air that think differently. In a way, the *World Report* is the only original program that you have this."[52]

## GMA-TV7, Philippines

Karen Davila, a reporter for GMA-TV7 in the Philippines and a *World Report* contributor, said the CNN connection helped her get inside to cover a story that received great play in the international press. Sara Balabagan was a domestic worker who had gone to the United Arab Emirates to seek employment. She was raped, after which she stabbed and killed her employer. Her death sentence was commuted under great international pressure and, after a year, she returned home to Manila. Davila recalled that

> I was there assigned to do the story for the station I work for. There were all these big journalists grabbing for a one-on-one interview that same day. I have to admit I was feeling I won't get this, that type of thing. So what I did was, I passed through the kitchen door in the back and immediately saw Ambassador Roy Seneres, he's the Filippino ambassador to the UAE. I said, "Sir, I'm Karen Davila, I know we've never met. . . ." He says, "No, I know you. You're famous." I'm like, "Huh? My local program gets to the UAE?" And he says, "No, I see you on CNN." He freaked me out.

---

[52] Simone Duarte (foreign editor, TV Globo), interview (October 1996).

We talked about it, then he told me, "Yeah, you can have the one-on-one interview." So I got it.[53]

## STAR-TV, Greece

Demi Hadji is a reporter for Star-TV, Greece, and said she began submitting news items to *World Report* because she thought it was important that the world get a more complete view of issues affecting Greece from the point of view of the Greeks. The international news agencies seemed always to present the news from the point of view of an outsider. According to Hadji,[54]

> The international news agencies are the basic source of international news which informs us, yet, the *World Report* is a significant source for one to understand how each nation views a thing concretely. Of special value to me is the opportunity which arises when *World Report* airs two reports on the same topic. For example, when the confrontation arose between the Greeks and the Turks over the Greek island that the Turks wanted to claim. I was happy when *World Report* used both pieces, mine and the Turkish one. That way, the people throughout the world can see both sides of the story and arrive at their own conclusions.
>
> At the station where I work, there does not exist censorship. I pick whatever events I consider to be relevant or of interest so that the television viewers all over the world can see them. This is what I send. Rarely do I pick some political story except if it affects Greece, or if it involves some controversy relating to a foreign land, as in the case of the Turks. I avoid those stories because I feel that the internal politics of one nation does not concern other nations. I try to select soft news themes which will show the distinctive character of Greece, to help foreigners acquire a taste of Greece, to have them become acquainted with her even though she may be thousands of kilometers distant.[55]

---

[53] Karen Davila (reporter, GMA-TV7 Philippines), interview (August 1996).

[54] Demi Hadji (reporter, Star-TV Greece), interview (July 1996).

[55] Ibid.

Hadji is typical of a group of contributors who, if they wish to send reports in to *World Report,* must do it on their own time and sometimes at their own expense.

> The problems which I face are many. First, because I am not paid for the *World Report* stories I produce, I must do them in my own free time. There is no way I can do them during my work hours at the station, at least not officially. Writing, shooting, and editing therefore must be performed after hours. The station cannot offer me a crew so I am obliged to make 10 or more stand-ups all at one time so that I will have enough to use in all the reports submitted over a three-to-four-month period. That is why sometimes it seems a bit comical when I make a report on the fires in the forest while the stand-up is in front of the Acropolis and I am well dressed and all made up.
>
> Also I am often obliged to take work which someone else has reported, which means that I am working on secondhand material. If the reporter has not done a good job, has not conducted a good interview, then I am not able to do the kind of job I would like to do. I prefer to have been in the place where the story takes place. I prefer to do the interviews myself and all the other work involved. In relation to sending the reports to Atlanta, from the moment that I have produced the report and it is ready, at least two days are required.
>
> I appreciate the *World Report* because it gives me the possibility of seeing firsthand what is taking place throughout the world. I like the reports as they are presented without any intervention from the international news agencies. The local stations can present their stories as they want them. Clean straightforward content. I too wish to understand the precise meaning of what happens, to know the conditions of the country, what the government wants to do [if the story has been sent from a national channel]. I especially like reports concerning people from lands which I do not know, learning how the people live there and their customs. I like also very much when there are special reports. For example, to see how a wedding takes place in 20 different lands, and how funerals are conducted, and so on. [56]

---

[56] Ibid.

## CMT-TV, Venezuela

The Turner idea that television can and should be used as a force for good has its proponents among the contributors, many of whom are attracted to the *World Report* for that very reason. These are the journalists who follow principles of "development" or "civic" journalism, a constructive approach to helping solve community problems using the media—whether print or broadcast—to give voice to signs of hope.

Debra Daugherty pointed to Fernando Jauregui, the *World Report* contributor from CMT-TV, as a member of a media movement in Latin America that uses development journalism to further its purposes. "He is unique," she said. "Very altruistic. *World Report* is his venue."[57] According to Jauregui, the basic reason he contributes is that

> *World Report* is a window to show the world what is happening in Venezuela. I do a special kind of journalism called journalism for development. The basis is that you try to report positive things of the society. Society, [of] which the government is a part, accomplishes many things. When you have to talk about something negative, what you do is, besides point out the problem, you also point out who is working to solve that problem or show what it is possible to do to solve that problem.
>
> That way, to an international audience, I can tell them from my point of view—through the view of journalism for development—what is happening in Venezuela. In many ways, that helps you to bring pressure on government institutions to do what they have to do.[58]

As an independent producer with clients all over the world, Jauregui has his own equipment and has worked for the international television service, World Television News (WTN), as a freelance shooter. He has worked for Kuwaiti TV in Venezuela, and had recently completed a one-week assignment in the Amazon with a French agency producing a documentary on native

---

57 Fernando Jauregui (CMT–TV), interview (August 1996).

58 Debra Daugherty (assignment editor, *World Report*), interview (August 1996).

AL PARTNERS

NN *Special Reports* staff had referred Jauregui
Daugherty.

*Report* as a labor of love. He went and sought
ɔadcaster willing to work with him. He pro-
ł Spanish-language *World Report* on his own
d the anchor links for the Ritual Special [the
program on rituals around the world] in
Spanish in the jungle, in the Amazon—it's a perfect setting
for it.[59]

Jauregui works for a broadcaster who is not a CNN client. But, according to Daugherty, his contributions to *World Report* have prompted his station's competitor—and one of CNN's biggest clients in Latin America—to start contributing to *World Report*. For Jauregui, contributing to *World Report* is less about competition and market forces, and more about trying to improve society.

> I have, I believe, a very powerful and special social tool, which is news. *World Report* is for me the opportunity to tell, with no censorship, without offending anybody, without being aggressive with anybody—I have no restrictions to say what I want to say—to the people of the world. Sometimes that converts into very specific actions that help people in these countries, especially those people who are in a struggle to make democracy work better, to respect human rights, and also to let people know the good things about Venezuela, which is a country in crisis, but where people are trying to work it out.
>
> I will give you a very specific example. I did a report on the regional elections for governors and mayors and other local authorities of last December 3. I had sent a report saying how traditional politicians and parties are against decentralization of power because most of the power is being held by the president and by party authorities. In a way that is very centralized. In Venezuela, it is only very recently that you can vote for your own governor. Before, the president will choose the governor for each state.
>
> I was complaining about that traditional system of politicians and parties. At the same time, I expained that non-government organizations were working to facilitate

---

[59] Ibid.

the process of decentralization of power. I began with something negative—the fact that there is resistance to decentralization. On the other hand, I was pointing out what was being done to solve this problem. And showing, through the report, that the government institutions that take care of the elections in this country had officially approved the participation of observers from these non-government organizations to check out that there is not any fraud in the elections.

As a result of the report, these non-governmental organizations were able to participate officially with the permission of the government. In those places where these people were observing, there was less fraud than normal. That allows me to help the people who don't have the chance to be on the air. To let the pople know. I believe that when other people in other countries similar to Venezuela see the same situation, they can learn from what is being done in Venezuela. They can watch through the reports I do.

First, if people really believe I am not getting paid, with the few exceptions of people close to me, they would think I am stupid. They won't believe I do so much work. It's not only the number of reports I send. It's how much I put into them. I mean each of them for me is important so I do sound mix and everything. I really put a lot of heart into it, and they won't believe I am not getting paid for it. Actually, when people see me on CNN they think I am making a lot of money out of it, [while in truth] I am putting money out of my own pocket for the CNN *World Report* in Spanish because it is of value for me.

It's like having the satisfaction . . . of giving some people in Venezuela an alternative in information. It makes me feel good because it's like wanting a country to be better. Instead of preaching about how bad it is, you go and try to do something about it. [CNN *World Report* in Spanish] is one of the ways I have to do it. I hope eventually it will make some money for me.[60]

Jauregui said he enjoys some aspects of his work for WTN, including the competition that is part of broadcast journalism; but

---

[60] Jauregui, interview (August 1996).

he does not always enjoy the grim realities of the hard-news arena.

> Most of the times I do bad news. For example, the last breaking news I did was a riot in the jail where 26 people died by fire. I called to say this is happening, I can cover it and I will interview the security forces. [The WTN people] said "Well, we don't want it, if it's just a story from outside the jail." But they found out that AP and Reuters were going to do it so they wanted me to do it. "Did you get any pictures of the bodies?" they wanted to know. I said "No, so far nobody has been able to do it. . . ." The kind of news most of the time they want is not very nice news and, because I work for WTN, I am one of the ones that sends bad news from Venezuela.

> For me, it's more important the fact that I can be a voice for Venezuela for the good and the bad things, to criticize or to help, even though some of my criticism may hurt the country. . . . We need to report that because we think it has to be covered and needs to be changed. We are going to touch very delicate points, very negative points, but we are also showing what is being done or can be done to change the situation, [hopefully encouraging] normal people [to] get involved in government business when education is a social problem.[61]

## Affiliate–Contributor Convergence

When CNN sent its fully-equipped newsgathering team to cover the hostage crisis in Lima, Peru, in effect it was demonstrating how the task of gathering news internationally can operate in a cooperative, win-win-win environment. The affiliate station, TV Asahi, benefitted from CNN's commitment of resources as much, if not more, than did CNN itself. Indeed, TV Asahi had full access to the equipment, anytime, day or night, even ahead of CNN's own reporters. CNN made no money by providing the service to TV Asahi, but certainly solidified the 15-year partnership it has had with the Japanese broadcasting giant.

---

[61] Jauregui, interview (October 1996).

The same equipment that TV Asahi and CNN reporters used also was used by *World Report* so that one of its contributors, Josefina Townsend from Peru's Monitor TV, could provide a live update on the hostage crisis for the Sunday *World Report* program. Townsend, who has contributed more than 70 reports since she began with *World Report* in 1991, also had been stringing for CNN Spanish (expanded and renamed CNN en Español in March 1997).[62]

In her accompanying videotaped report, Townsend profiled Nestor Cerpa, one of the leaders of the hostage-takers. Townsend's taped report and live Q&A with *World Report* Anchor/Executive Producer Ralph Wenge, illustrated how the newsgathering efforts of *World Report* contributors already project themselves onto CNN air, albeit within the context of the *World Report* program. The fact that the satellite feed was available to the *World Report* program reflected the change in how CNN managers view the program as a vehicle for breaking news *and* analysis. The convergence in Lima, Peru of CNN, TV Asahi, and the Peruvian contributing station illustrates how the viewers of news around the world can benefit when news organizations and journalists join forces to cover the news.

---

[62] Susan Winé, interview (January 1997). The program aired on January 6, 1997.

NEWS REPORTS ARE SENT OUT *to 210 countries and territories around the world, and in the United States, as well, from the CNN International studio and newsroom. In fact, today CNNI has 85 million subscribers – even more subscribers than CNN has in the United States. CNN International has been in service since 1985, but has experienced most of its growth since the Persian Gulf War. Currently, there are approximately 16 live broadcasts daily from this studio that go to Europe, Asia, Africa, the Pacific and North America. CNNI newscasts also come out of Washington, London, New York, and Hong Kong. As at CNN and Headline News, the anchor desk is open to the newsroom, allowing us to use this working newsroom as the backdrop to the anchor desk, and to bring the viewer right inside the immediacy of the newsroom environment.*[*]

---

[*] http://cnn.com/StudioTour/StudioTour6.html

# 8

# The International Audience

*Throughout the Iraqi occupation, CNN was being monitored in
Kuwait City by the Iraqi forces and by Kuwaitis who were resist-
ing the occupation. There was a woman who was able to watch
CNN in her house. She was a resistance leader. Still, this woman
called us. She had a satellite telephone in her house. Then they
[the calls] stopped coming. We knew and the woman knew there
was great risk in calling CNN to give these eyewitness accounts.
We found out after the war had been concluded that the Iraqis had
actually tracked her down and tortured her to death for the crime
of calling CNN and giving her eyewitness account. I was sick.*[1]

Zola Murdock sits in the middle of the newsroom. Surrounding
her are the noise and activity of journalists talking on telephones,
news writers working at computers, news anchors consulting on
scripts, assignment editors ordering satellite feeds, and, peering
down from the catwalk above, the visiting public touring One
CNN Center, Atlanta. As director of Public Information at CNN,
Murdock oversees a staff that spends its days answering telephones, responding to faxes and e-mail, and working through
stacks of cards and letters that pour into CNN Center every day.

Murdock is strategically situated between the National and
International Desks, which are the primary newsgathering operations in the expansive CNN newsroom. Her location is more than
just a symbolic gesture to communicate CNN's interest in

---

[1] Eason Jordan (senior vice president, CNN), quoted in Wayne Walley, "CNN
International Chief Tells Tales From Global News Front," *Electronic Media* (27
June 1994): 4.

listening to its audience. Viewers can alert CNN journalists to stories they don't yet know about, especially breaking news stories. CNN news managers also know that viewers are quick to recognize a mistake. If any detail — in a name, a title, or a place — that goes out over the air is incorrect or misleading, CNN viewers will be the first to relay the mistake to the network. And given CNN's round-the-clock operation, corrected information — whatever the source — can be integrated into the story the next time it airs, according to Stephen Cassidy, a manager on the International Desk.

> The nice thing about TV is that, if you make a mistake in a newspaper and they flop that newspaper up on your front step, that mistake lives for 24 hours, until the next newspaper arrives. But if we make a mistake on CNN, well maybe we can fix it next hour and in hours thereafter. We are more organic.[2]

Murdock's Public Information department in Atlanta consists of six people, but as many as 30 people a day may be working telephones and answering mail. She hires mainly CNN staff — typically VJs ("video journalists") — to work overtime. Working hours are 7 A.M. to 10 P.M. but during times of intense news activity, such as the aftermath of the Olympic Park bomb explosion, the telephones are staffed 24 hours a day. On August 14, 1996 — a fairly typical day — her report for the day shows that CNN received 840 telephone calls, 116 pieces of mail, and 920 items online. Each contact is counted and logged. Every member of Murdock's staff turns in a report each day, from which a daily summary is prepared and hand-delivered to the executives. A copy circulates to all staff through the company's internal computer network. Murdock also prepares a weekly cumulative report, which is sent to Ted Turner and a select group of company managers.

Feedback from viewers outside of the United States is summarized in a separate daily international report, which is prepared by one of Murdock's staff members, Dana Caghan. In her report for August 17, 1996, Caghan wrote:

---

[2] Excerpted from comments made to CNN's International Professional Program participants (September 1996).

President Clinton received happy birthday wishes from abroad. A viewer from Belgium said, "It is is a very special day today. Today Clinton is 50 years young. We also believe on the occasion of this special day that such a young, dynamic and strong president will remain in power at least for another four years. One commented, "I can't believe Clinton is still going to have a party when his people were killed today."[3]

Also noted in the report was the apparent uproar over Germany not allowing the showing of the movie *Mission Impossible* because of actor Tom Cruise's religious affiliation; a viewer from Holland wrote:

> Not only Germany but other countries too have recognized that there is more behind the Scientology Church. Some journalists in Europe have discovered that high ranked members had ties to Satanic cult groups. In Germany and the Netherlands critics say that Scientology members have infiltrated German and Dutch organizations.

Terrorism was very much on the minds of some viewers who, growing frustrated with the slow pace of the TWA 800 investigation, developed strong feelings about what they saw on television:

> We know who supports terrorism, we know where they are trained and training. We know what countries they reside in. We know who are the financial backers and we just sit and do nothing about this. It is time for not turning the other cheek and remedy the problem at the root. Terrorism has no place in a civilized society and should not be tolerated. My stomach turns thinking such violent actions can go on in America.

Even seemingly mundane topics like the weather — more specifically, weather reports — can trigger reactions from viewers. An American in Quatar complained that "CNNI has stopped mentioning any weather about the U.S. I prefer CNNI, and watching the BBC for weather reports is not my 'cup of tea,' so to speak." Another, from Holland, wrote that "I would like to see the

---

[3] Referring to the U.S. military C-130 crash in Jackson Hole, Wyoming.

forecast for North America and Asia back on the program."
Wrote another:

> After talking to business travelers and fellow airline pilots,
> we really miss the U.S. Weather map. Also, the other inter-
> national weather maps, far east, India, etc. that were broad-
> cast in the past were invaluable resources.

From her listening post in London, Murdock's colleague, Sarah
Maude, receives and responds to telephone calls, faxes and letters, mostly from the U.K., Europe, and North Africa, regions that
take CNN International's European satellite feed. "The biggest
controversy we have at the moment—believe it or not—is the
change in the policy on the world weather," according to Maude.

> [The CNN executives in Atlanta] took an editorial decision
> recently to only do the weather for the area that particular
> feed covered, rather than the world weather. I was inun-
> dated, because the sort of person who watches CNN Inter-
> national is very often a traveller or someone who is an
> [expatriate] or who has relatives in another part of the
> world. I happen to know I wasn't the only feed who got the
> complaints; other feeds got them too, since it was a world-
> wide decision.

> I had to explain [to viewers that] it was an editorial
> decision. Then, [CNNI] brought out a program called
> *American Edition* which is on three times a day, that is three-
> quarters of an hour long, and has American weather in it.
> We have picked that up. If somebody wants Stateside
> weather, I can at least tell them to watch *American Edition*.
> But we have a lot of people in the U.K. who are Asian or
> have family in Asia. They can no longer see what the
> weather is doing in that part of the world, or for Australia
> or New Zealand, and they don't get it any more. They say,
> "When are you going to change it?" I explain that it is not
> my brief to change it. "I will pass your comments along."[4]

Sometimes, even the job of listening has to be explained to viewers, as well as CNN's views on the limited power of television,
according to Maude.

---

[4] Sarah Maude (public information department, CNN), interview (January 1997).

> My proviso to them always has to be: "My brief is a listen-
> ing brief. I have no editorial authority." They talk to me and
> I pass it along to the relevant authorities. I do not express an
> opinion and I do not say anything will or will not happen.
> Mine is a listening and passing-on brief.

Maude said viewers will call her office, convinced that she has a
direct link to each and every one of CNN's writers and editors,
and that all she has to do is to tell them to take care of whatever
concerns the caller. Often a viewer will launch into a long dis-
course, which goes far beyond the particular story that triggered
the call, wanting to explain the history of the area or what happened last week, just to insure that CNN is getting the overall
picture. Or better yet, that it changes its news coverage to reflect
the views of the caller.

> What they cannot understand, having rung us up and given
> us the information, and having gotten me to say I would
> pass it on, is why three weeks later things are exactly the
> same. Then they ring me back. All I can say is, "Well, it's
> not up to me. I [will pass] your comment on again."

More frustrating still are the calls from viewers who seem to believe that CNN is part of the U.S. government.

> During the [U.S.] election, people called up saying, "Why
> don't you tell President Clinton . . . " or, "Why don't you tell
> Senator [Bob] Dole . . ." I had to explain that we are a tele-
> vision company. We have no affiliation with the present
> United States government or any future United States gov-
> ernment. We wish to maintain our independent status. . . .
> The only time when I can absolutely and totally refute
> something is when it is hinted that we are associated with
> any particular government or are receiving money or are
> influenced by any government in the world. Then, I have to
> refute that and state our independence.[5]

But coverage of hot-button topics, or even of certain regions
like the Middle East, inevitably results in contacts from viewers
who are convinced that CNN *does* trade in opinions — and always
the *wrong* ones, from the viewer's standpoint;

---

[5] Ibid.

> If you ring up, for instance, and say, "[You] had a piece which was so pro-Zionist, I don't know why you and all your offices don't just go and live in Israel," I can almost guarantee you that the next caller will be somebody saying "You are so pro-Arab, are [you] the paymasters for some Arab nation?" [But] we always feel that if we get complaints from both sides then we must be doing something right.[6]

Maude's London operation reflects the realities of internationalization, in that she—and CNN—must abide by local [i.e., United Kingdom] protocol, even in the area of viewer feedback.

> Public Information here [in the U.K.] is not the same as in the States. We are required by law under the Independent Television Commission to have what they call a "complaints procedure." We answer a range of queries, we take complaints and comments and we log them under the law for the U.K. But then I deal with them in the way that will fulfill the service requirements of CNN International.[7]

Maude said that CNN's attention to viewer feedback is not just a matter of fulfilling the law, but in fact reflects the company's respect for its international audience.

> We have certain phrases that we use in our letters which reflect the attitude of CNN International to its viewers. One of them is that we obviously wish to maintain the highest journalistic standards, therefore appreciate it when people take the trouble to call or write, even if it is as minor as a caption under a photograph that was wrong. Sometimes when the graphics department isn't as knowledgeable as the journalists, they get a territory wrong, so somebody rings up to say, "You have got the Pakistani part of Kashmir in India." Then I can sort that out. I can get in touch with the graphics department and get them to make sure the borderlines are done correctly. . . . The thing I love about the job is that practically every single contact that is made has to be approached in a different way. You cannot conveyor-belt it. Every letter that we write may have certain phrases in it—because it reflects our philosophy—but every letter will be individual. I can almost guaranteee you that, were you to

---

[6] Ibid.

[7] Ibid.

pick up two letters from two different viewers, you would not say this is the same letter. Or this is the same telephone call. Every query is approached on an individual basis.[8]

## Personal Relationships

One day during the spring of 1996, a viewer in Dahran, Saudi Arabia telephoned the CNN International Desk in Atlanta. The caller said he had heard on a military shortwave radio channel of an explosion at the U.S. military base and wanted to know more about it. Once the assignment editors working at the International Desk concluded it was not a prank caller, they started calling official contacts in the Saudi and U.S. governments to see what they knew or would tell. The assignment editors even called hotels within visual range of the U.S. base, hoping to get reactions or statements from persons who may have seen or heard the explosion. On determining that an explosion had in fact occurred, and that it was not an accident, the International Desk mobilized CNN personnel to the scene from various bureaus and from Atlanta. A local journalist in Dahran was hired, another journalist was sent from Riyadh, and phone reports from eyewitnesses were arranged. All this was done within minutes of the initial call from the CNN viewer in Dahran.

Almost simultaneously, an e-mail message arrived at CNN Center from a writer who identified himself as being associated with CIA operations in Saudi Arabia. He begged that his message be treated confidentially, but he nonetheless wanted CNN to know that a bomb had gone off at the U.S. military base in Dahran.

Many in the network's audience want CNN to win. That is to say, they want CNN to have access to the latest news, and to portray accurately and cover completely the news, whatever and wherever it is. These viewers take the time to call long-distance to Atlanta—usually at their own expense—or e-mail detailed information to the newsroom because they have come to see CNN as part of their extended family. They believe CNN wants to hear

---

[8] Ibid.

from them and will take what they have to say seriously. Maude said she observes this phenomenon every day.

> You are sitting in your home watching it, maybe with one or two other family members or by yourself, or in a hotel room or wherever. . . . It is not like a cinema where you go into an audience situation. . . . I come from a theatrical background and I have discovered that people have different ways of approaching actors depending on which medium they are in. If they are in television, very often [television viewers] look upon them as a personal friend. I actually have friends who have been in sitcom after sitcom, series after series, and total stangers will come up to them in the middle of the street and start a conversation with them as if they were a personal friend. Because they are in their living rooms every evening.[9]

CNN Senior International Assignment Editor Stephen Cassidy wishes that everyone who works at the network could be required to work in Murdock's Public Information department at least one day every year.

> I think we should all be in a position to take those calls. It's harder to be arrogant if people are coming around asking about this mistake and that mistake. We make mistakes all the time. We're human beings, this is a human organization.[10]

Even prior to the inauguration of CNN Interactive, CNN networks and their specific programs were making a conscious effort to involve their audiences and elicit viewer feedback. On CNN's domestic service, *Talkback Live* and *Larry King Live* actively solicit viewer participation in the program, as does CNNI's *Q&A*, with Riz Khan. Other forms of interactivity with viewers included contests in which viewers sent in answers to questions such as the location of UNESCO World Heritage sites pictured but not named in the program. Responses came in from all over the world.

---

[9] Ibid.

[10] Stephen Cassidy (senior international assignment editor, International Desk), from comments made to CNN's International Professional Program participants (September 1996).

The advent of e-mail has made it possible for television news programs to receive a steady flow of viewer responses, and in the case of *World Report* and other programs that air on CNN International, the feedback comes from any locale that is served by e-mail facilities and receives the CNN signal. The e-mail correspondence received by the *World Report* staff indicates that many viewers see the program as part of CNN's international news-gathering operation. Wrote a viewer from London:

> If you could get a camera and reporter in to reveal the government-caused suffering of ordinary citizens in the north [of Sri Lanka], it would truly be a scoop that CNN is so famous for. . . . The government is banning food, medicine, gasoline, electricity from its own citizens. They have refused to let the Red Cross or reporters into the area.

From the *Independence*, which at the time was steaming once again to the Persian Gulf, came an offer from a U.S. sailor to help:

> Like to send out a big thanks for the quality coverage of the intensifying situation on our side of the planet. As you well know, things are still up in the air. Should you have any questions about the situation as it progresses, feel free to ask.

And from Saudi Arabia, this offer:

> I just wanted to fax you what I have here about the 'Mad Cow' disease treatment that was discovered by this Saudi nomad who said he could treat this vicious disease by some herbs that are available in the desert. I see no need for going to contractors for such good news that will save Britain billions of dollars!

Other helpful offers come in response to specific reports on the program:

> Some weeks ago I saw a report on CNN depicting the plight of widows rejected by their deceased husband's family. I was quite moved by this story in part because I am a widower, and recently lost the last remaining member of my family. I am very interested in making some kind of contact with either the reporter/editor responsible for the story, or the women's rights agency in India.

s were equally willing to go the extra distance to help
*port* improve its international coverage. A woman from
...un, desperate to correct CNN's misperceptions about Taiwan, offered to *World Report* Executive Producer Ralph Wenge "to pay your United Airline ticket and 5 days hotel rooms in Taipei" so Wenge could attend the inauguration of the Taiwanese president following the general elections.

Like the Taiwanese woman, many correspondents are hoping to encourage *World Report*—and sometimes CNN on the whole—to do a better job of covering the writer's country or region. A Kenyan viewer admonished CNN to

> focus your broadcasts to support environmental issues and the concept of the common planet, that we all belong to the same earth . . . In Africa, leaders take CNN seriously. They get embarrassed if their actions are broadcast around the world on CNN. The focus for Africa should be on human rights, fighting corruption and supporting positive role models. My country's leaders are better behaved today because of CNN!

A viewer from Israel wrote,

> How simple it is to convey the Lebanese as the victims and the Israelis the horrible perpetrators. How untrue and unjust to all of the people involved. CNN has a moral responsibility to evaluate what it screens for more integrity, professionalism, and honesty. Those people in your organization should be held accountable for presenting the most primitive propaganda as "news." How do you justify this?

Other suggestions for improvements were somewhat more down-to-earth, if not entirely relevant to *World Report* itself. "Please could you bring *Style with Elsa Klensch* more often and please include more African attire," wrote a Kenyan viewer. And from Pakistan, a suggestion that applies to much of television itself: "Please don't interrupt [*World Report*] so much with a lot of ads."

# Audience Feedback

During late 1996, the authors surveyed approximately 200 *World Report* viewers who had written by e-mail to *World Report*.[11] Although the recipients of the e-mail survey do not constitute a representative sample of *World Report* viewers, given their access to e-mail and the fact that they were self-selected, the authors were able to learn more about the issues they had raised in their communications with *World Report*.

The e-mail survey asked viewers to give their impressions of the *World Report* program, to indicate where and how often they viewed the program, to make suggestions for improving the program, and to assess how important the program was, from their personal perspective. About 40 questionnaires were undeliverable due to incorrect or nonfunctional addresses. Approximately 100 usable responses were received, some with quite lengthy comment, almost all appreciative of the opportunity to have their say.[12] The responses illustrate the range of opinions and views in those responses.

# Likes

Many of the e-mail respondents included positive comments, such as the one from an Islamic student attending university in the United States:

> *World Report*'s mission to bring viewpoints to our attention unedited is commendable; and largely it has been successful in this regard. Particularly, I appreciate it when one foreign country will do a piece on another country. One such recent example was a Portuguese segment on returning refugees in Bosnia.

From Charlottesville, Virginia, a viewer wrote that

> There are always two sides to every coin. In real-life situations, we are often given news slanted to one side or an-

---

[11] E-mail address: world.report@turner.com

[12] Don Flournoy, "E-mail Study: CNN *World Report*," Institute for Telecommunications Studies (Athens, OH: Ohio University, December 1996).

other. Since this has become an integral part of making news sound more interesting, we need to hear views of all people or groups involved. . . . I love the way *World Report* splashes in nice, happy things related to different cultures and societies. Having a proper mix of good and bad news is an important part of successful communication.

A priest working in El Salvador wrote:

I love listening to the native reporters and seeing their countries. I understand some of it has to be censored or modified at the source but even that is useful. . . . I am a Korean War veteran, a chemist with patents and publications, who in a different time might have been a historian. But CNN exemplifies what I teach in my classes. Television is one of the best inventions of man. It enables us to see each other in real time and with minimal interference. I would appreciate it if [CNN] would use its pulpit to also teach.

# Dislikes

Some viewers saw stories they did not like, oftentimes expressing worry that contributed reports could do harm. A viewer from the United Kingdom wrote,

I find it hard to watch propaganda dressed up as news. As some of the television stations are owned and staffed by government ministers, a bit of editorial comment to state this would not be amiss. . . . For evidence of what happens if you broadcast unbiased news see the BBC World Service who were removed from Saudi Arabia for daring to suggest that the country is not a democratic state.

A viewer from Pakistan wrote that,

While I do appreciate CNN's efforts to telecast "uncensored" news clips from various countries, it is nauseating to see Pakistan Television's government-oriented propaganda on your network. . . . The Pakistani segments on *World Report* are reducing CNN's credibility among Pakistani viewers.

An international student attending the University of Michigan wrote that, even though he is favorably impressed with *World Report*,

> I still think that CNN's claim to be an international channel is rather dubious. . . . International news coverage is scarce in the U.S. I have found European news coverage to have a much better international flavor. While CNN covers the U.S. well, it does not come close [in its international coverage] to the BBC and various European news organizations.

A viewer from North Carolina had a similar reaction:

> *World Report* fills a very important need in today's world, especially in America. As more and more broadcasts are becoming more specialized and they are marketing to specific groups, our diversity becomes a dividing force. . . . After I spent a few months in England, I was disappointed by the lack of original foreign broadcasts that could be received in the U.S. Foreign news perspectives were almost unheard of. Many American broadcasts tried to attract an audience by claiming to be from a "global perspective." Instead, they only had a global backdrop. CNN *World Report* is a refreshing break from the norm.

## Segmenting Audiences

In the *CNNI – Beyond 2000* planning document, CNNI's Chris Cramer outlined for fellow members of the CNN Executive Committee and for the CNNI staff his ideas for the future of the international channel. About the audience, he noted that

> Recent audience research for CNNI has shown what we have known for some time—that the channel outperforms all other news and news-related channels in all demographics. Our recent suggestion that viewers should fax or e-mail us their thoughts about our programming has been phenomenally successful. Those messages demonstrate to me on a daily basis that the audience is engaged and vocal about all that we do. We need to respond to as many of their concerns and wishes as we can. We have a loyal and

> enthusiastic audience who take world affairs seriously and expect us to do the same.[13]

Finding out precisely who is watching CNNI is not an exact science. Certainly there is a passionately loyal—if small—group of viewers who follow the CNNI signal from hotel to hotel as they travel from place to place around the world. There is another group of people who have been dispatched—perhaps for years at a time—to locations around the world, who work for embassies, NGOs (non-governmental organizations), and commercial enterprises of all types. These are highly literate English speakers, they are reasonably affluent, and they exhibit a high level of interest in international affairs.

CNNI has a much larger, but more diffuse, regional following, made up of a group that CNN describes as "influentials." In two 1995 studies, conducted for Turner News Research by the Center for International Strategy, Technology and Policy at the Georgia Institute of Technology, the target group for "influentials" included cabinet level ministers, deputy ministers, chiefs and former chiefs of defence, a vice-chief of defence, a chairman of a joint chiefs of staff, legislators, military service chiefs, a government spokesperson, corporate chairpersons, CEOs, company presidents, corporate vice presidents, ambassadors and former ambassadors, senior policy officials, secretaries general, a president of a national association, a university president, and religious leaders.[14]

The Georgia Tech studies concentrated on Europe and Asia. In Europe, the approach consisted of 154 personal interviews conducted between January and September, 1995, in France, Germany, Italy, Netherlands, Norway, and the United Kingdom. Not

---

[13] Studies by the AGB/Intomart/Netherlands for Europe in the first quarter 1996 showed that CNNI was outperforming NBC Superchannel in all demographics; the International Air Travel Survey for Asia during early 1996 conducted by European Data & Research Ltd. showed CNNI leading the field in the "viewing of channels by region" when comparing CNBC, ESPN, ABN, BBC World, and CNNI (except that BBC World (39%) led CNNI (29%) in India.

[14] "Influential Europeans/Asians Study: Ad Sales Analysis," Center for International Strategy, Technology and Policy (Atlanta, GA: Georgia Institute of Technology, 1995).

surprisingly, typical "influentials" in Europe represent an (45+) segment of the viewing audience. Most received CN cable (74.3%) or satellite dish (15.2%). Also not surprising is that nearly half of the viewers report watching CNNI in their hotel room while travelling (43.9%);[15] nearly one-third watch at home (31.1%); the remainder mostly watch in their office (23.7%).

Influential Europeans reported being frequent viewers of CNNI, according to the findings. More than half reported watching the channel more than three times per week (30.6% watch it five to seven days per week, and 24.6% watch it either three to four days per week. Nearly one in five viewers watch it one to two days per week (17.1%). The remainder reported watching it at least once a month (22.4%). A vast majority (85.6%) said they watch CNNI more frequently during coverage of major news events.

For the Asia study, 106 personal interviews were conducted in Hong Kong, Singapore, Taiwan, and Thailand. As was the case with influential Europeans, typical "influentials" in Asia represented an older segment of the viewing audience. Smaller percentages received CNNI via cable, while the rest received the channel via satellite and over-the-air antenna. The percentages of this population that watched CNNI at home, at the office, and in hotel rooms when travelling were almost identical.

Who the "non-influentials" are — the "average" home viewer of CNN International — is not yet measured, nor likely to be anytime soon, given the expense and the lack of interest on the part of CNN and its competitors. These companies are more interested in the high-end viewer, because even if the numbers in the audience are small, they represent a demographic that appeals to advertisers. According to Lynne Gutstadt, vice president for news research at CNN, the company's target audience internationally is, in fact, at the high end of the economic scale:

> We still are looking at relatively limited distribution. There's no point in [determining viewership] in the bottom 50 percent of the socio-economic when they don't have

---

15 79.3% of the Europeans surveyed said they prefer hotels with CNNI, while 78.5% of the Asians surveyed said likewise.

access to CNN. In fact, it's a much larger group than that. As an English language service, it's probably always going to be targeted at a relatively small percent of the population in the countries where we're distributed.[16]

"Influentials" bring economic leverage and economic clout. In other words, they have money. The spend it on business and personal travel, computers, cars, and the like. Unlike the mass audiences in the United States, who offer advertisers the chance to sell great quantities of inexpensive merchandise items, the CNNI audience in Europe and Asia can afford luxury goods at premium prices.

CNNI *does* have a North American audience, but only an estimated 2.4 million cable subscribers receive service that includes CNNI. A weak satellite signal can only be picked up by large, backyard satellite dishes of the analog (C-band) type, a declining market of 3.6 million potential households. Some (but not all) of the backyard dish packages offer CNNI as an option, but in 1996 that offering was halved as distributors introduced the new business-oriented CNN*fn*, which now fills the daylight hours of that channel.[17]

The assumption seems to be that CNNI will not find a market in the United States, where CNN and CNN Headline News — the network's so-called "domestic services" — are well established and where carriage space on cable channels is at a premium. CNNI, along with other niche programs, awaits the opening of new capacity that distributors hope and assume will come with the introduction of digital cable and digital satellite.

The part of the U.S. audience that wants *more* international news undoubtedly are frustrated with the network's new niche programming strategy, which has decreased the exposure American viewers have to international news material on the network, and which may go down still more in the future. It already has happened. The afternoon *International Hour*, which incorporated a daily *World Report* segment, was replaced by *Talkback Live*, the

---

[16] Lynne Gutstadt (vice president for news research), interview, January 1997.

[17] Rich Brown, "All the News That's Fit to Transmit," *Broadcasting & Cable* 126 (24 June 1996): 50.

interactive talk show hosted by Susan Rook. The 6 P.M. *WorldView* program, produced jointly by CNN and CNNI, is the only program that airs on all of CNN's U.S. and international feeds simultaneously, and is the only significant international program available on a daily basis on either of CNN's domestic services.[18]

These programming decisions are based on market research, which indicates that Americans are not interested in international news. While CNNI's Chris Cramer defended the company's commitment to international news coverage, he acknowledged that the research did not point to a demand for much international news on U.S.-based channels;

> Ted [Turner] and Tom [Johnson] believe that the audience in this country *should* get a fair proportion of its international news, and they won't stop doing it. But they're not helped by the audience research. The audience research is quite the opposite to that, which is a terrible shame.[19]

When asked about Ted Turner's comments on the U.S. viewer, given at the 1996 *World Report* Contributors Conference, when Turner called the American people "stupid," Cramer said that Turner was more than a little frustrated with his fellow Americans' apparent lack of interest in the rest of the world.

> He does get very angry and I understand why. The audience out there is not stupid. Maybe it's what they've been fed. Maybe it's because they've been fed this over a long [period of time]. . . . I mean, none of the people I know in this country are stupid. Many of them have an avid appetite for the *New York Times* and *Wall Street Journal*, that kind of thing, so why can't that translate to television?[20]

But Bob Furnad, executive vice president for CNN, said he is convinced that Americans are uninterested in what goes on around the world because of their geographic isolation.

> People in this country don't care what goes on in the rest of the world. There are reasons for that. We are far different

---

18 A fifteen-minute version of *World Report* airs at approximately 3:15 A.M., eastern time.

19 Chris Cramer (vice president, CNN International), interview (September 1996).

20 Ibid.

than the nations of Europe, for example. We are an island with nothing but friendly neighbors close by. You look back at the time of the Cold War. We had missiles as close as Turkey to the Soviet states. We raised hell when they tried to put missiles in Cuba, and when they didn't, we were here very secure. There was no threat that was immediate until long-range missiles were created. We were isolated. That geographic isolation has created a feeling of isolation on the part of the citizenry and how world news affects them.[21]

Furnad noted that many American viewers are only interested in international news when it involves the lives of Americans.

If an American life is in danger and the story is out of Africa, they are going to care about it. If the story is out of Africa and it involves millions of non-Americans, people are not going to care about it, even though it is their tax money that will be spent to send food and military aid over. But until our American soldiers set foot there, they are not going to care about it. It is a huge danger.[22]

Ironically, it was not marketing/audience research alone that has caused CNN's domestic services to cut back on their international coverage in search of better ratings. Earl Casey, vice president and managing editor of CNN national news, conceded that the advent of CNNI itself caused CNN and Headline News to become even more American in tone and focus.

We still provide, depending on what the day's news flow is, international news coverage. But I think that definitely, for the CNN service, there has been a conscious decision to make it more of a national broadcast with international material in it. It's impossible not to . . . so it's fairly rich in that regard. Of course we do a one hour newscast a day on CNN which is simulcast on all of the networks—the 6:00 program.

There's international news throughout the day, but I think if you talk to the producers of those networks, they did decide to do that, particularly when CNN International itself is such a robust service for international news. The

---

[21] Bob Furnad (executive vice president, CNN), interview with Paolo Ghilardi (November 1996).

[22] Ibid.

odd thing about this is, CNN International now has a program that really is about the United States. We call it *American Edition*. . . . But you have to think also of all the news stories that are just international by definition. Financial coverage, technology, medicine, all of that *is* international as long as the scope of your reporting embraces the international [dimension].[23]

Richard Roth, CNN's United Nations correspondent and host of CNNI's weekend feature program, *Diplomatic License*, acknowledged that CNN's use of international news material in its U.S. programming is down, if not entirely out: "[On CNN-domestic] they are going more for the American audience and hope that by hooking them they can slip in international news here and there."[24] But, given the realities of the marketplace, Roth said he sees the situation getting worse before it gets better.

It's all factionalization, sectionalization. I would like to see more international news on CNN but it's not happening. It's happening less and less. I don't even get seen domestically. It's overseas that I am seen.[25]

CNNI's Cramer also would like to see more international news on CNN's U.S. services, even in the face of audience data that indicates a lack of viewer interest: "I think CNN needs to be courageous, but I can say that because I work for CNNI and I don't have to look at the ratings." One day the need for ratings services among international television services may increase as advertisers demand reliable audience data. As the competition among the services grows, the need will be acute. Once audience numbers are available from more and more markets around the world, the inevitable push to boost CNNI ratings could be the catalyst that forces producers at CNN International to create television news that appeals to the world's many *local* audiences.

---

[23] Earl Casey (vice president and managing editor, CNN), from comments made to CNN's International Professional Program participants (September 1996).

[24] Richard Roth (United Nations correspondent, CNN), interview (December 1996).

[25] Ibid.

CNN HAS HELPED BY MAKING *what is a U.S. news medium reflect different perspectives by using local contributors. . . . We hope you can assist in sustaining and nurturing peace and freedom by your hawk-eyed vigilance in exposing repression, injustice and oppression to make the world inhospitable to them. You have assisted the various struggles for justice and freedom by depicting those struggles and their almost inevitable outcome when dictators and other authoritarian and unjust rulers have been shown to bite the dust and to do so comprehensively. The spectacle of a successful struggle in one place has been subversive of injustice and oppression elsewhere. It has served to encourage those pitting their strength against great odds. You can be a great moral force for good. You can demonstrate that this is a moral universe, that right and wrong matter, that however long it may take, however high the cost, justice, truth, and goodness will ultimately prevail. It is impossible for evil, injustice, oppression and exploitation to have the last word.*

### The Most Reverend Desmond Mpilo Tutu[*]
Archbishop of Cape Town, South Africa

---

[*] Excerpted from comments given to the *World Report* Contributors Conference, Atlanta, Georgia (28 January 1992).

# 9

# The Third Age

*To measure our success in the year 2000, it means continued influence, it means more viewers – even more than the current 115 million households that we get into. This may seem like a strange objective, but in the battleground which is called Europe, continued coverage, and continued exposure for us . . . is a real objective. And it's not a defensive objective. There's so much competition in Europe. That's got to be a real objective. In Asia, the objective is to significantly extend our reach into those parts of the world like India and China, where, frankly, it's a bit feeble at the moment. So if we approach the year 2000 having achieved all of that, I think we will have done quite well.[1]*

In early January 1997, crowds of Bulgarians gathered to voice their opposition to the Socialist government, began chanting, "Where is CNN? Where is CNN?" Eager for international attention, they impatiently questioned the delay in news coverage they clearly expected. "Do we have to tear down the Parliament to get on CNN?" they shouted. They were not disappointed. A few days later the CNN crew sent from London arrived. When one of the rally speakers spotted CNN Correspondent Christiane Amanpour standing in the crowd, he called out, "Christiane Amanpour is here! Come up and speak to us!" The crowd roared its approval. Amanpour declined the offer, staying in the crowd to cover the story.[2]

---

[1] Chris Cramer (vice president, CNN International), interview (January 1997).

[2] Story relayed to the International Desk by Julietteter Zieff (freelancer contracted by CNN to cover the story in Sofia, Bulgaria), January 1997.

Ted Turner's vision—and his audacity to act on it—has created a company that, while American in many respects, has taken on an international mission. The same vision that created the company has subsequently driven it to embrace bold innovations in its use of technology, in its approach to the news and information business, in opening market opportunities, and in its willingness to use its influence to be a communicator for peace, justice, and protector of the environment. For Turner and his companies, the process of innovation nearly always begins by trying to avoid the trap of conventionality.

> I was in [my] office and had been looking at Antarctica [on my globe] for some reason. And I had the world turned upside down. I had the Southern Hemisphere on top. And somebody came in and came over here and turned the world over. And I said [to him], "What are you doing turning it over!?" He said, "Well, you've got it upside down." And I said, "Absolutely!" So I thought about it. I think about things that other people don't think about. First of all, about 80 percent or 90 percent of all the land mass in the world is in the Northern Hemisphere. But out in outer space, there is no up and down. And people standing in Antarctica, they're just as much up as we are! The only reason that the world has always been portrayed on maps with the Northern Hemisphere on top is because the map makers were from the Northern Hemisphere.[3]

Turner readily accepted the premise that how news was produced also was a reflection of the fact that the news producers of the world were from the western world. Eason Jordan, who oversees CNN International, once noted that it was Turner's wish to have a CNN bureau in every country, to make sure that news from every corner of the globe could get into the news mix.[4] The creation of *World Report*—a clear break with convention that went against the advice of people he had hired to run his news company—was a step in that direction. Local broadcasters in the international arena had been long ignored. As CNN aspired to become a source of international news, it needed the news that local

---

[3] Ted Turner (vice chairman, Time Warner), interview (December 1996).

[4] Wayne Walley, "CNN International Chief Tells Tales From Global News Front," *Electronic Media* (27 June 1994): 4.

*affect layout*

stations could provide, or at least their help in getting access to the stories that CNN reporters would cover. More often than not, the local stations were flattered when CNN came calling. They also needed a reliable source for international news, and were happy to know that a big-name company like CNN wanted them as partners.

CNN has been very good at cultivating clients and affiliates, in many cases providing introductory offers of access to its international feeds free or at greatly reduced cost. In 1987, CNN invited local stations around the world to submit stories to its global newscast, *World Report*, and shortly thereafter created the Atlanta-based International Professional Program. Contributors also could attend the annual *World Report* contributors conferences in Atlanta. In these ways, a geographically, politically, religiously, and culturally diverse group of media were brought into the CNN family.

More than ten years later, the network's partner stations around the world are not only getting their own reports onto CNN air, but they are helping the company achieve more comprehensive coverage than it otherwise could, even if contributors and affiliates are unlikely ever to supplant the international newsgathering staff that now provides the network's newscast producers with international news for their shows. Ironically, *World Report* has operated in near anonymity. Its existence is known mainly to those stations and their correspondents who contribute, to those viewers who have happened upon it, and to occasional supporters and critics. In total there are an estimated 200 participating broadcast organizations, but fewer than half could be considered active at any given time. While the ratings of the *World Report* newscasts are no better or worse than CNN/CNNI programs in comparable time-slots, *World Report* is not universally appreciated within CNN, either as a newsgathering apparatus (mainly because of the uneven quality of the reports that appear on the program and their occasional blatant lack of balance) or for its internationalizing influence.

But the *principles* reflected in *World Report do* pervade CNN, and thus internationalize it. Like other Turner initiatives that began as public service gestures, *World Report* over time has come to be seen as a smart business strategy. From all indications, *World Report* was not begun with that intent, and does not today operate from a profit motive. Instead, *World Report* embodies the working principles of idealism, trust, broad participation, mutual coopera-tion, and multifaceted partnerships that make for fast, compre-hensive, diverse coverage in the news business. It just so happens that these principles are good business, and have worked to favor the Turner company internationally. CNN management clearly is behind the program and what it is trying to accomplish. The rea-son CNN airs "unedited uncensored" news and perspectives, and works hard to see that they are properly framed and as close in production quality as possible to its own product, is because it recognizes that a world of news exists that no one else is covering, that news can, and often does, have more than one point of view. It also helps that the relationships and the entrée it gives CNN into every region of the world are keys to its global competitive-ness.

Certainly, telecommunication technologies have helped the Turner companies find an audience by extending their reach. CNN's 24-hour news channel was first made available domesti-cally by satellite, and later, satellites enabled it to become a news broadcaster to the world. Satellites figure prominently in CNN's plan to regionalize its services according to Cramer:

> It ought to be possible in the next year or so to begin utiliz-ing low-earth orbit satellites, which means you really could start to produce television programming for different parts of the world, at much less cost. I have a gleam in my eye, but no more than that, that we might get to regionally in-jected advertising, regionally injected programming, so eve-rything doesn't have to be rather clumsily uplifted from Atlanta. That kind of technology is just around the corner.[5]

Digital technologies, in the form of computer-based communi-cations and the Internet, now are permitting a redefinition of the traditional concept of news broadcaster and newscast, with in-tentional communities of viewers forming around Web sites ca-pable of by–passing established news providers altogether. Audi-ences are now able to make their own contributions to the mix of

---

[5] Cramer, interview (January 1997).

"unedited uncensored" news, very much as *World Report* has done, to comment on the news, and to screen and tailor news to their preference. In this sense, the *World Report* initiative forshadowed and prepared the company for the open communication and the Internet.

CNN Interactive is the company's "experiment station," a test-bed for news in the on-line world. CNN management, not knowing where cybernews is going, is putting scarce company resources into the venture to at least stay ahead of the curve, and, when possible, set the form for others to follow. As with the company's traditional television networks, CNN Interactive will be able to rely on the CNN brand and an aggressive entrepreneurial spirit to carry it into whatever form the new medium takes.

## The Future

The company's international success also is its curse. CNN's managers know they are no longer playing in a field of one. Imitators will strive to equal or surpass the American news company's global reach. CNN watches, but doesn't wait for the growing list of its competitors to overtake it. Many of the same managers who brought the network to U.S. and later international prominence now work to keep it at the forefront of the global news business, not by merely replicating old ways that helped create and define the company, but by seeking new ways to appeal to the audience for news. The competition already is forcing the network to reexamine fundamental strategies regarding global versus niche programming, and the process is not always comfortable.

Cramer, hired specifically to make CNN's on-air product more appealing in the increasingly competitive international market, said that CNN's strategy must include programs of the type that it has been known for, along with new programs that expand the network's repertoire:

> We're not prepared to wither on the vine. We have to, whilst maintaining what we're good at, build on what we're good at and we have to put on additional programming which is "appointment viewing." Which gives the audience

a second or a third reason to tune in. And that's the strategy which underpins what we're doing. What we're trying at the moment is laying side by side with what we're good at, a compendium of other programs, which gives the audience several other chances to tune in. In other words, "value-added" [programs].[6]

What works on CNN's U.S. newscasts — that is, showing news that focuses mainly on the domestic news agenda — will now become more evident in other markets served by CNN International. Already, vernacular programming is being planned, which means that CNN will one day be delivered in local languages rather than just in English. The bottom line, according to Cramer, is getting people around the world to watch CNN, and that means being more *international* from an American standpoint, but more *local* from the standpoint of the viewers in other parts of the world:

The criterion for me, on or around 2000, is "Do we have an international news and information channel?" — although I'm more likely to say, "Do we have a *series* of news channels?" Because later this year we'll be splitting the signal for CNN International into regional feeds — large parts of it day and night. So that we can address the four distinct marketplaces we have — Latin America, Europe (which includes Africa), Asia, and North America. So at the year 2000 the yardstick I will use is, "Do we have an international news and information channel which is regionally sensitive and regionally specific at those times of day when it suits, when it's appropriate and makes good sense?" The best formal yardstick is, "Are we still as influential then as we are now?" And the yardstick for me will be that we are even more influential. And at the same time I would use the word "relevant." "Are we, in those marketplaces, even more relevant than we are now? Even more compelling? Even more engaging? And even more 'must view'?"[7]

To meet the information needs of the global market, CNN inevitably inevitably makes the news. Creating news programs that are compelling and relevant to a global audience means that

---

[6] Ibid.

[7] Ibid.

CNN must report on important events whenever and wherever they happen. In doing this, the network continues to expand its role as global communicator, the channel for diplomats and generals — even angry crowds in streets and town squares — with the potential to shape public life in every corner of the planet.

# Bibliography

Alter, Jonathan. "Ted's Global Village." *Newsweek* 115 (11 June 1990): 48–52.

Armstrong, Robert. "Global Introduction: An Analysis of Singapore's Initial Contributions on CNN's *World Report*." *Sojourn – Journal of Social Issues in Southeast Asia* 9 (October 1994): 246-259.

Arnett, Peter. *Live from the Battlefield*. New York: Simon & Schuster, 1994.

_____. "Peace, War and Global Communication." An Elizabeth Evans Baker Lecture, Ohio University, Athens, Ohio (26 April 1996).

Brown, Rich. "All the News That's Fit to Transmit." *Broadcasting & Cable* 126 (24 June 1996): 50.

_____. "Fox Unveils News Channel Lineup." *Broadcasting & Cable* 126 (9 September 1996): 47-48.

Bulloch, Chris. "BBC Goes Commercial on a Global Scale." *Via Satellite* (August 1994): 14.

Burns, Nicholas. "Talking to the World about American Foreign Policy." *Harvard International Journal of Press/Politics* 1 (Fall 1996): 10-14.

"Buyouts Shuffle 1985 Media Rankings." *Advertising Age* (30 June 1986): S-4.

Charity, Arthur. *Doing Public Journalism*. New York: Guilford Press, 1995.

"CNN Digs Its Claws In: Raymond Snoddy Meets CNN News Group Chairman Tom Johnson." *Financial Times* (9 December 1996): 19.

"CNN to Begin Broadcasts in Moscow By End of Summer." Reuters (6 May 1989).

Colman, Price. "TCI Will Carry Fox News Channel." *Broadcasting & Cable* 126 (1 July 1996): 48.

Cortese, Amy, and Rob Hof. "Network Meets Net." *Business Week* (15 July 1996): 68–70.

Cramer, Christopher, and Sid Harris. *Hostage*. London: J. Clare Books, 1982.

Dawley, Heidi. "The BBC as We Know it is Signing Off." *Business Week* (12 August 1996): 50.

Dawson, Greg. "Closer Terms as the World Turns." *The Record* (24 February 1988): E22.

Dickson, Glen. "BBC Worldwide Television." *Broadcasting & Cable* 126 (18 November 1996): 80.

Dilawari, Rani, Robert Stewart, and Don Flournoy. "Development Orientation of Domestic and International News on CNN *World Report.*" *Gazette* 47 (1991): 121-137

Fallows, James. *Breaking the News: How the Media Undermine American Democracy.* New York: Pantheon Books, 1996.

Fleming, Heather. "The No News Convention." *Broadcasting & Cable* 126 (19 August 1996): 8.

Flournoy, Don. "Monday Memo: A Global News Commentary." *Broadcasting* 115 (20 November 1989): 25.

_____. *CNN World Report: Ted Turner's International News Coup.* London: John Libbey and Company, Ltd., 1992.

_____. "E-mail Study: CNN *World Report.*" Institute for Telecommunications Studies. Ohio University, Athens, Ohio. December 1996.

_____. "The Developing Story of Cable's International News Coverage." *Broadcasting* 114 (22 February 1988): 66.

Flournoy, Don, and Chuck Ganzert. "An Analysis of CNN's Weekly *World Report* Program." *Journalism Quarterly* 69 (Spring 1992): 188-194.

Flournoy, Don, Debra Mason, Robert Nanney, and Guido Stempel III. "Canadian Images of Canada: U.S. Media Coverage of Canadian Issues and U.S. Awareness of Those Issues." *The Ohio Journalism Monograph Series.* Athens, OH: E. W. Scripps School of Journalism, Ohio University, 1992.

Freed, Ken. "MSNBC Interactive Merges TV, Web." *TV Technology* (29 November 1996): 29.

Friedland, Lewis. *Covering the World: International Television News Services.* New York: Twentieth Century Fund, 1992.

*Global Forum* with President Clinton." The Carter Center's Day Chapel, Atlanta (3 May 1994).

Goldberg, Robert and Gerald Jay Goldberg. *Citizen Turner: The Wild Rise of an American Tycoon.* New York: Harcourt Brace & Co., 1995.

Goodman, Anthony. "Ted Turner Blasts U.S. Veto, Rival Murdoch." Reuters Financial Service (22 November 1996).

Grover, Ronald. "Murdoch vs. Everyone." *Business Week* (9 December 1996): 75-79.

Haddad, Charles. "CNN Hires No. 2 Man from BBC." *Atlanta Constitution* (8 February 1996): E1.

Hall, Jane. "A News Voice For The Third World; CNN's *World Report* Celebrates Its Fifth Anniversary with a Two-Hour Retrospective on Sunday." *Los Angeles Times* (24 October 1992): F1.

Hall, Lee. "Arch-Conservative to Host Fox Cable Show." *Electronic Media* (26 August 1996): 32.

_____. "Breaking Live: A Moment of Truth for TV News." *Electronic Media* (7 October 1996): 32.

_____. "The Man Behind the Man." *Electronic Media* (9 December 1996): 38.

Hammer, Joshua. "Triumphant Ted Turner, the Swashbuckling Media Visionary Brightened Our Hopes for a Global Village." *Playboy* 37 (January 1990): 76–77+.

Hodges, Ann. "Clinton to Take a Grilling from the World." *Houston Chronicle* (3 May 1994): 4.

_____. "It's Unanimous: CNN a Major Player; Broadcasters from Around World Agree on Network's Clout." *Houston Chronicle* (7 May 1994): 6.

"Influential Europeans/Asians Study: Ad Sales Analysis." Center for International Strategy, Technology and Policy, Georgia Institute of Technology, for TBS International (1995).

Johnson, Carla Brooks. *Winning the Global TV News Game.* Boston: Focal Press, 1995.

Johnson, Debra. "Westinghouse/CBS Gets Global Cable Foothold." *Broadcasting & Cable* 126 (1 July 1996): 14.

_____, and Nicole McCormick. "News Corp. In India." *Broadcasting & Cable* 126 (16 September 1996): 59.

Knight, Robin. "Global TV News Wars." *U.S. News & World Report* 117 (26 December 1994): 70.

Kongkeo, Rachada. "A Content Analysis of CNN *World Report*: Development News from Non-Western Perspectives 1987-1988." Masters thesis, Ohio University (1989).

LaFayette, Jon. "Fairness Will Set Fox News Apart." *Electronic Media* (9 September 1996): 3.

_____. "Granath's Grand Tour: Longtime ABC Exec To Be Feted for Role in TV Around the World." *Electronic Media* (26 November 1996): 12.

Lee, Sangchul, and Ece Algan. "CNN World Report: A Five Year Analysis." Research Monograph. Institute for Telecommunications Studies. Ohio University, Athens, Ohio. January 1997.

Loory, Stuart. "News from the Global Village." *Gannett Center Journal* 3 (Fall 1989): 165–174.

MacBride, Sean. *Many Voices, One World*. Paris: UNESCO, 1980.

"Making War and Keeping Peace: What Should Television Report?" The Baker Peace Studies Program, Ohio University, Athens, Ohio (26-27 April 1996).

Mandli, Murtaza. "U.N. Chief Warns of North-South Technology Gap." Inter Press Service (22 November 1996).

McClean, Lisa, and Robert Stewart. "The Caribbean Story on CNN *World Report*: In Search of 'Development News.'" *Gazette* 55 (1995): 55-67.

McClellan, Steve. "Telenoticias on the Grow." *Broadcasting & Cable* 126 (16 September 1996): 38–39.

_____, and Rich Brown. "Cable News Prepares for War." *Broadcasting & Cable* 126 (24 June 1996): 44–50.

McConville, Jim. "MSNBC Blocks Headed Overseas." *Broadcasting & Cable* 126 (5 August 1996): 63.

Mermigas, Diane. "Murdoch Vows Action Against Time Warner." *Electronic Media* (23 September 1996): 1, 30.

_____. "The Murdoch Map." *Electronic Media* (7 October 1996): 6.

_____. "Time Warner-Turner Merger's First Effect Likely Seen Overseas." *Electronic Media* (7 October 1996): 46.

Merritt, Davis "Buzz." *Public Journalism & Public Life: Why Telling the News Is Not Enough*. Hillsdale, N.J.: Erlbaum, 1995.

Mowlana, Hamid. *Global Communication in Transition: The End of Diversity?* Thousand Oaks, N.J.: Sage Publications, 1996.

"MSNBC Aims to be 'Net News Mag." *Broadcasting & Cable* 126 (24 June 1996): 45.

"News Corp. to Launch JSkyB." *Japan Times* (13 June 1996): 14.

Nickson, Daphne. "Reunions for Dissidents." *South China Morning Post* (15 February 1993): 8.

Park, Chun-il, Rani Dilawari, and Don Flournoy. "Development Orientation of Domestic and International News on the CNN *World Report*." Research Monograph. Institute for Telecommunications Studies. Ohio University, Athens, Ohio. 1992.

"Peace Prize: Belo OK, but Horta? No Way!" *News and Views of Indonesia*, Republic of Indonesia, Directorate of Information. Jakarta, Indonesia (October 1996): 1-2.

Range, Peter Ross. "The Demons of Ted Turner." *Playboy* 30 (August 1983): 62–63.

Rohter, Larry. "In Trying to Get Into Cuba, CNN Hits Snags at Home." *New York Times* (13 January 1997): D1.

Rosen, Jay. *Getting the Connections Right: Public Journalism and the Troubles in the Press.* New York: Twentieth Century Fund, 1996.

Rosenstiel, Tom. "The Myth of CNN." *New Republic* 211 (22 August 1994): 27–33.

Scroggins, Deborah. "'We Did It! We Did It!' CNN Chief Says Scoop's The Thing, Not Famous Pen." *Atlanta Journal and Constitution* (29 December 1991): A6.

Shister, Gail. "CBS News Solidly in Third Place." *The Record* (2 July 1987): E13.

Shuster, Scott. "Foreign Competition Hits The News." *Columbia Journalism Review* 27 (May 1988): 43–45.

Slater, Lydia. "The Ingenue Who Couldn't Wait To Go to War; Christiane Amanpour Is the World's Highest-paid Foreign Correspondent." *Daily Telegraph* (27 June 1996): 13.

Snyder, Alvin A. Warriors of Disinformation: American Propaganda, Soviet Lies, and the Winning of the Cold War. New York: Little, Brown and Company, 1995.

Stilson, Janet. "CNN Steps Up Global Push in Persian Gulf War's Wake; Cable News Network to Open Far-flung News Bureaus after Covering Persian Gulf War." *Multichannel News* (29 July 1991): 3.

Strobel, Warren P. *Late-Breaking Foreign Policy.*Washington, D.C.: United States Institute of Peace Studies, 1997.

_____. "The CNN Effect." *American Journalism Review* 18 (May 1996): 33-37.

"Turner Slams Murdoch in Address to U.N. Panel." *Daily Variety* (25 November 1996): 14.

Usborne, David. "Murdoch Meets His Match; Ted Turner, Founder of CNN, is Taking Him On in New York." *Independent* (24 November 1996): 15.

Veal, Sarah. "CNN Passes Around the Mike." *International Herald Tribune* (11 May 1994): Finance section.

Walker, Martin. "Nation Speaks Unto Nation — Via CNN." *The Guardian.* (4 May 1994): 9.

Walley, Wayne. "BBC World Coming to U.S." *Electronic Media* (1 January 1995): 33.

_____. "CNN International Chief Tells Tales From Global News Front." *Electronic Media* (27 June 1994): 4.

Walley, Wayne, and Jon LaFayette. "ABC Cable News Good as Dead." *Broadcast & Cable* (27 May 1996): 1, 23.

Warren, James. "CNN Show Offers a Motley, Manipulated Look at World." *Chicago Tribune* (4 March 1990): 1

Weaver, James B., Christopher J. Porter, and Margaret E. Evens. "Patterns In Foreign News Coverage on U.S. Network Television: A 10-Year Analysis." *Journalism Quarterly* 66 (Summer 1984): 356-363.

Weisman, Adam Paul. "As Ted Turns." *New Republic* 195 (29 December 1986): 16–17.

Whittemore, Hank. *CNN: The Inside Story*. Boston: Little, Brown and Company, 1990.

Yu, Xinlu. "What Does China Want the World to Know: A Content Analysis of CNN World Report Sent By the People's Republic of China." Unpublished paper. Presented to the Radio-Television Division of the Association for Education in Journalism and Mass Communication. Washington, D.C., August, 1995.

# Index

## A

ABC, 1, 21, 112, 134, 137, 170, 173
APTV, 68
ATM (multimedia) data line, 135
Abu-Khudair, Abdul, 36
advertising, 2, 5, 83, 109, 197–98,
    201, 206
Afghan Media Resource Center
    (AMRC), 165
Afghanistan, 96
Africa, 5, 12, 16, 21, 25–26, 43, 45,
    67, 69, 73, 76–77, 84, 103, 110,
    117, 119–20, 149–54, 158–59, 173,
    182, 186, 192, 200, 202, 208
Ailes, Roger, 142
Alatas, Ali, Indonesian Foreign
    Minister, 131
Albright, Madeleine, 45, 47
Algan, Ece, 23n
Alter, Jonathan, 28–29, 35
Amanpour, Christiane, 44, 47, 62,
    66–67, 203
*American Edition*, 119, 186, 201
Amorim, Paulo Henrique, 171–73
Angola, 96, 154, 158–60, 173
apartheid, 149, 152
appointment viewing, 207
Arab perspective, 17, 67, 78, 87, 132,
    174, 188
Arafat, Yasser 45, 89
Argentina, 33, 71, 170–71
Arnett, Peter, 20–21, 59–60, 64, 87
Artear Channel 13, Argentina, 170–
    71
Asahi National Broadcasting
    Company, Ltd., 68, 143, 145–49,
    166, 180–81

Asia, 5, 11, 22, 69, 73, 99, 110, 113,
    117, 119–20, 136–37, 140–41, 143,
    182, 186, 196–98, 203, 208
Asia Business News, 117
Asia TV Ltd., 11
AsiaSat, 140
ASkyB satellite service, 141, 143
Associated Press (AP), 59, 85, 93,
    142, 180
Atlanta, Georgia, 5, 8, 10, 12, 20–21,
    33–34, 40–47, 51, 67, 69, 71–75,
    82, 85, 89, 93, 95, 97, 99, 103, 105,
    109, 115, 117, 125, 129, 145–47,
    152, 154, 158–59, 161, 167, 172,
    176, 183–84, 186, 189, 202, 205–6
*Atlanta Journal and Constitution*, 21
Australia, 14, 117, 141, 143, 186
Australian Broadcasting
    Corporation, 153
Aziz, Tariq, 102

## B

BBC (British Broadcasting
    Corporation), 13, 30, 45, 70, 115,
    117, 124, 129, 131, 138–40, 167,
    185, 194–95
    Arabic TV service, 131
    public service orientation, 139
BBC Worldwide Television, 139
Baghdad, 7, 59, 64, 102
Balkans, 47
Baltic countries, 76
Barnett, Libby, 146
Bayrak-TV–North Cyprus, 161
beepers (phone reports), 63, 69, 73,
    81, 86, 101, 103
Beijing, 7, 31, 44, 53, 100, 106
Beirut, Lebanon, 69, 119
Belarus, 76
Belgrade, Yugoslavia, 67
Belize, 75, 144, 169
Belo, Carlos Ximenes, Bishop, 131
Bernknopf, David, 44n
bias, in news coverage, 17, 43, 48,
    51, 72, 142
Birt, John, 139
Biureborgh, Leif, 158–59
Bosnia, 9, 60, 62, 65–66, 159, 193

Role of internet -
digital?

Technology → . conv.